# PRAISE FOR
# *PROFESSIONAL SE*
# *LEADERSHIP HANDBOOK*

'It is not uncommon to be elected or appointed to a leadership post without a real understanding of the many challenges that the role will throw up and with little support on hand to guide you along. The *Professional Services Leadership Handbook* will be a lifesaver for people in this situation. Based on the authors' collective professional and personal experiences, it is written in a clear and entertaining style with lots of invaluable practical advice.'
**Anne-Marie Piper, Senior Partner, Farrer & Co**

'This eminently practical handbook guides successful professionals on how to build the additional personal competencies they need to stand out as effective leaders. Through a robust interview process with industry leaders, as well as their many years of collective consulting experiences, the authors present a series of thoughtful frameworks and a synthesis of well-constructed leadership lessons. It all amounts to a really useful companion for those who have committed themselves to making the challenging personal transitions ahead – tomorrow's leaders!'
**David Bowerin, former Head of Strategic Marketing, Citigroup**

'The *Professional Services Leadership Handbook* is an excellent tool for future and experienced leaders operating in a dynamic and ever-changing business-to-business environment, where differentiation is a critical success factor, and where leaders often misunderstand how to lead. This is a must-read handbook.'
**Michelle Jones, Chief Communications and Investor Relations Officer, CH2M**

# Professional Services Leadership Handbook

How to lead a professional services firm in a new age of competitive disruption

Nigel Clark, Ben Kent, Alastair Beddow and Adrian Furner

KoganPage

First published in Great Britain and the United States in 2017 by Kogan Page Limited

| | | |
|---|---|---|
| 2nd Floor, 45 Gee Street | c/o Martin P Hill Consulting | 4737/23 Ansari Road |
| London | 122 W 27th St, 10th Floor | Daryaganj |
| EC1V 3RS | New York, NY 10001 | New Delhi 110002 |
| United Kingdom | USA | India |

www.koganpage.com

© Nigel Clark, Ben Kent, Alastair Beddow and Adrian Furner, 2017

The right of Nigel Clark, Ben Kent, Alastair Beddow and Adrian Furner to be identified as the authors of this work has been asserted by them in accordance with the Copyright, Designs and Patents Act 1988.

ISBN       978 0 7494 7734 9
E-ISBN   978 0 7494 7735 6

**British Library Cataloguing-in-Publication Data**

A CIP record for this book is available from the British Library.

**Library of Congress Cataloging-in-Publication Data**

Names: Clark, Nigel, author. | Kent, Ben, author. | Beddow, Alastair, author.
Title: Professional services leadership handbook : how to lead a professional services firm in a new age of competitive disruption / Nigel Clark, Ben Kent, Alastair Beddow and Adrian Furner.
Description: 1st Edition. | New York : Kogan Page Ltd, [2017] | Includes index.
Identifiers: LCCN 2017027253 (print) | LCCN 2017022499 (ebook) | ISBN 9780749477356 (ebook) | ISBN 9780749477349 (pbk.)
Subjects: LCSH: Service industries–Management. | Professions–Marketing. | Leadership.
Classification: LCC HD9980.5 (print) | LCC HD9980.5 .C53 2017 (ebook) | DDC 658.4/092–dc23
LC record available at https://lccn.loc.gov/2017022499

Typeset by Integra Software Services, Pondicherry
Print production managed by Jellyfish
Printed and bound by CPI Group (UK) Ltd, Croydon, CR0 4YY

# CONTENTS

**01 Vision: how to create and implement a robust strategic plan** 13

**02 Innovation: how to reap the benefits of innovation in your firm** 34

# LIST OF FIGURES AND TABLES

## Figures

## Tables

# ABOUT THE AUTHORS

## Nigel Clark

Nigel has both led and advised professional services firms for more than 20 years and is currently the Global Head of Marketing at SLR, an environmental and advisory services firm. He is also a non-executive director of PSMG and the editor and lead author of the *Professional Services Marketing Handbook*, published by Kogan Page.

## Ben Kent

Ben is the Founder and Managing Director of insight-led consultancy Meridian West. Ben advises many of the world's leading professional and financial services firms on their client engagement and provides strategic research, consultancy and training for professional firms.

## Alastair Beddow

Alastair is a Director at Meridian West, working with professional and financial services firms of all sizes to develop and implement engaging, differentiated and successful client-focused strategies, business development initiatives and thought-leadership campaigns.

## Adrian Furner

Adrian is Managing Director of Kommercialize, the practitioner-led advisory firm focused on commercial excellence. Adrian has held senior corporate leadership positions in which he was responsible for commercial, procurement and operations, acting as both a customer and a supplier of a diverse range of professional services.

# PREFACE
## Your practical leadership handbook

Professional services leadership comes in many guises: it is possible to be a leader of an office, a practice area, an industry sector group, a business services team or even a whole firm. However, these various leadership roles all have one thing in common: they offer important, exciting and surprising challenges that are materially different from the responsibilities and challenges faced by professionals who focus their time on delivering work to clients, managing delivery teams, or developing new business from clients. Leadership is a real step change and one that should not be underestimated.

If you are reading this book then you have probably already built yourself a successful professional career in a professional services firm. Now you may have decided that you want to achieve greater impact within your firm by taking on your first leadership role, or you may have made the transition to leadership already and therefore want to increase your effectiveness, or to move to the next stage of your leadership journey. This book can help you in any of these scenarios.

To be a successful leader you need to develop a new mix of skills and insights that extend far beyond your technical capabilities. We have written the *Professional Services Leadership Handbook* to provide practical guidance on the major leadership challenges facing professional firms and to help professionals accelerate their personal leadership development. It contains common scenarios, issues and challenges encountered by professional services leaders and practical solutions, best practices and frameworks to guide your thinking towards a leadership approach that works for your circumstances. We recognize that there are already many 'business bibles' that explore generic concepts of leadership, which is why we have tailored the insights in this book to the specific experiences and needs of professional services leaders.

After a short introduction charting the challenges created by the disruptive landscape in which professional services leaders find themselves operating, we explore four themes on the agenda for any professional services leader. The book is divided into four parts comprising three chapters each. First, how to lead your firm as a business to create a strategy that will generate long-term, sustainable profits. Second, how to show true client leadership to create a client-focused culture in your firm that anticipates and responds to changing clients and markets. Third, how to lead the people in your firm to drive high performance and encourage greater collaboration. And fourth, how to take time to reflect on your self leadership to ensure you balance competing leadership priorities successfully. In the conclusion, we bring together the lessons learnt throughout the preceding chapters.

The book draws on our collective experience working within professional firms (as both fee-earners and business services leaders), within large corporates and as consultants to professional services firms, and on our own proprietary research. We combine this with insight from our extensive experience of speaking with clients of professional firms about how their relationships with external advisers are changing, and the steps leaders of professional firms need to take in response.

In preparing this book we have interviewed leaders from a range of professional firms, big and small, UK and global, about their route to leadership, what they learnt during their transition and how they respond to common leadership challenges. We share their experience and wisdom so you can learn lessons from leaders who have travelled a similar path to the one you are on now. We are grateful to everybody who has been generous with their time and insight, particularly those who agreed to be quoted directly in the book.

The leaders we spoke to say that it can sometimes be lonely at the top, with an ever-increasing list of demands and little time to reflect. Yet they also say that leading a professional firm can be an incredibly rewarding and motivating experience where the results of hard work and clear vision are tangible and plain to see.

Whatever your leadership journey, we hope this book will accompany you along the way. It is designed not only to be read from beginning to end but as a reference point you can turn to again and again when you need guidance or a refresher on a particular topic. We hope it becomes a well-thumbed and familiar friend.

# ACKNOWLEDGEMENTS

The authors would like to thank everybody who shared their time and insight to help make this book possible. This includes all friends, family and colleagues at Meridian West, Kommercialize and SLR, as well as the team at Kogan Page.

We would like to extend special thanks to all those people who agreed to be interviewed as part of the development of this book. This includes: Alan Hodgart (Hodgart Associates); Anna Gregory (Farrer & Co); Annette Müller (EY); Charlotte Jones (Grant Thornton); Christina Blacklaws (Cripps); Claire Nelson; Clare Singleton; Clive Stevens (Kreston Reeves); Deepak Malhotra; Ed Clark (Arup); Fiona Colthorpe (Allen & Overy); Gail Jaffa (PSMG); Gareth Mason; Gavin Davies (Herbert Smith Freehills); George Bull (RSM UK); Heather Benjamin; James Partridge (Thomson, Snell & Passmore); Joanna Worby (Brachers); John Parkinson (Coffin Mew); John Rowley (TPM); Jon Randall (Moore Stephens); Jonathan Fox; Julieanne Wilde (Baker McKenzie); Kimberly Bradshaw (Buzzacott); Louise Field (Bird & Bird); Mark House; Mark Jeffries (Mills & Reeve); Matthew Whalley (EY); Michael Samuels (Grant Thornton); Miles Brown (Coffin Mew); Natasha Owoh (Bird & Bird); Nick Holt (SR Search); Nigel Howlett (PwC); Nigel Shaw (Fisher Michael); Nigel Spencer (Reed Smith); Philip George; Prity Kanjia (Grant Thornton International); Richard Chaplin (Managing Partners Forum); Robert Duggan (Mourant Ozannes); Sannam Majidi (Allen & Overy); Sarah Ducker (Irwin Mitchell); Stuart Hopper (Dentons); Tim Dixon-Phillip (Service Reality); Tim Pullan (ThoughtRiver); Tina Williams (Fox Williams) and Vikki Bingham (GVA).

# Introduction

## Leading professional services firms in a new age of competitive disruption

*It is undoubtedly easier to be a good leader if you have enjoyed the benefits of good leadership earlier on in your own career. Learning from others is priceless. In my experience a lot of good leaders are intuitive in the way they go about leadership and they typically have a high degree of emotional intelligence as well. Aptitude and genuine commitment trump long-service and seniority. Simply being the most senior partner or the biggest biller has no direct correlation with being a good leader.*
ANNA GREGORY, KNOWLEDGE, LEARNING AND DEVELOPMENT
DIRECTOR, AND FORMER EMPLOYMENT TEAM PRACTICE AREA
MANAGER, AT FARRER & CO

*Visibility of the leader is key. Effective leaders walk the floors of their building; they are visible and accessible to others in the firm. Being a leader is all about the impression you create and the confidence you inspire in others. In my experience really good leaders celebrate success and they aren't shy of telling people when they have done a good job. Most leaders do a decent job of managing the numbers but only the best leaders manage behaviours to get the most out of people.*
TIM DIXON-PHILLIP, CO-FOUNDER OF CONSULTING FIRM SERVICE
REALITY, AND FORMER SALES AND MARKETING DIRECTOR AT EY

*In my mind being a leader in a professional services firm is very much like being the captain of a big ship. The waves change, the wind changes, the weather changes, one moment it is night and the next moment it is day. You constantly have to make little adjustments as the world changes around you. In my experience people in professional firms tend to think, Okay, we have set our strategic*

*direction and we will plough ahead for the next year. But actually, that does not work. Just like a ship's captain, a leader in a professional firm has to think constantly about the external factors and little changes that will influence how you get to your intended destination.*
KIMBERLY BRADSHAW, MANAGING DIRECTOR OF HR SERVICES AT BUZZACOTT

Has there ever been a more exciting, demanding and daunting time to be a leader of a professional services firm? As the business environment becomes increasingly global, complex and interconnected the need for professional advisers, who can guide their clients through this changing landscape, has never been greater. Emerging market growth, coupled with deregulation, offers significant opportunities for firms pursuing aggressive international growth. Ongoing merger activity within the professional services sector has enabled firms to combine professional expertise in new ways to provide innovative service propositions for their clients and dominate niche sectors in ways never seen before.

Yet, several powerful and disruptive forces combine to make the future less than certain for professional firms. New competitors, with radically different business models, are beginning to take market share from established professional firms and, as a result, are recalibrating expectations about the client and adviser relationship. Technology has altered how professionals work: automation and artificial intelligence require substantial investment and raise fundamental questions about the role and value of professional expertise and experience. A new generation of people entering the professions have very different expectations about what they want from their careers.

The net outcome of these various changes means there will be both winners and losers within the professional services sector in the future. Although overall demand for professional advice remains healthy, the profitability of traditional firms is under intense pressure. The pace of change is accelerating, not slowing down, and consequently the firms that rely on business as usual will find it increasingly difficult to sustain a position of competitive advantage in their respective markets. This means professional firms must find new ways to address the changing needs of their clients, re-engineer their operating models and articulate their points of differentiation in a better way if they want to ensure that they have a sustainable and profitable future.

The need for strong leadership in this new age of competitive disruption is clear. With so many potential threats and opportunities at the door, professional services firms need leaders with a clear strategic vision and the ability to implement tough decisions quickly. Whereas firms have, historically, tended to be rather inward-looking in the way that they define success and measure performance – profit per partner is a typical metric of success – to thrive in a disruptive future the leaders of professional firms must be much more outward-looking in their approach. Without strong leadership, firms risk being overwhelmed by changes to their clients and markets and therefore incapable of responding to changes happening around them.

However, there are structural and cultural factors that have traditionally made leading a professional firm particularly challenging. As partnerships, professional firms are inherently conservative in nature, typically valuing consensus over directional leadership. They prefer evolution to revolution, and shy away from potentially divisive decision-making that rocks the boat too vigorously. To compound the challenge, many people within firms have historically found themselves in leadership positions accidentally, not out of conscious choice, and so perhaps have lacked the skills and experience to be effective leaders. In many firms leadership qualities have not been properly valued, or leadership has been seen as synonymous with being an effective rainmaker, so the people with the strongest leadership capabilities have not been identified and promoted properly.

This leadership deficit is now being addressed. Over the last two decades the professionalization of leadership within firms has brought about many significant changes in the way firms are structured, how they measure performance and how they develop younger talent to unlock their future potential. But more needs to be done. The successful leaders we interviewed for this book have many different leadership experiences but they share one common trait: they recognize that to be successful they need to be adaptable, agile and forward-thinking in their approach. They have learnt that it is not sufficient to react to disruption as it occurs, that they must instead anticipate change and be prepared to alter their course in light of unexpected events. The firms that place the greatest value on leadership equip themselves in the best possible way to adapt to a disruptive future.

We have distilled the various challenges facing leaders of professional firms into a simple framework that we call the Leadership Triangle (see Figure 0.1). At the corners of the triangle are three core elements that leaders in professional firms need to factor into their thinking at all times: the firm's business (its strategy, economic model and innovation capabilities), its clients (its external relationships and client-focused culture) and its people (its internal collaboration, team performance and skills). At the centre of the triangle is a fourth leadership element: self leadership. This fourth component – comprising self-reflection and evaluation, and leadership style and behaviour – is critical for all professional services leaders to master because it boosts the effectiveness of leadership within the other three elements of the triangle.

We call this framework the Leadership Triangle because it guides how leaders achieve the outcomes they want from their leadership, and provides a tool for leaders to articulate their vision for the future of their firm. Adaptable leaders are able to view their firm through each of the four lenses of the Leadership Triangle simultaneously to gain a holistic understanding of the impact of their decisions. For example, addressing clients' desires for alternative business models will likely strengthen client relationships and provide an effective

**Figure 0.1**   The Leadership Triangle

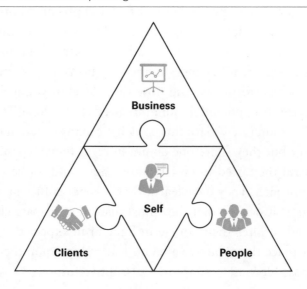

point of differentiation in the market, it but will also have an impact on the business in terms of short-term profitability because deploying new technology, or opening an offshore service centre, will require up-front investment. These moves will also have an impact on the firm's people because new delivery models will require new skills and new ways of managing client relationships and so will affect how a firm recruits and develops its people.

Adaptable leaders realize that the elements of the Leadership Triangle need to be kept in balance to avoid unintended consequences of ill-thought-through leadership decisions. Focusing on one element at the expense of others can instil the wrong kind of culture and behaviours within a firm. For example, if you focus too narrowly on business outcomes by boosting short-term profitability through increasing activity and hours worked, this will likely have a negative impact on people's engagement levels within the firm and, over a sustained period of time, on the quality of the service delivered to clients. In turn, a below-par client experience can damage client relationships, and so the short-term financial gains from increased activity may be offset by a decrease in client loyalty and a loss of recurring revenue from dissatisfied clients.

We use the Leadership Triangle, and the concept of balancing its four constituent parts, as the guiding principle for this handbook. In the 12 chapters that follow we focus on what we have identified as the major challenges for professional services leaders across business, clients, people and self leadership. Some of these challenges involve long-term strategic changes, while others are focused on the here and now of making a firm's existing operations work more efficiently. All are critical to leadership development and success, and all require a new, adaptable approach to leading professional firms into an uncertain and disruptive future.

# PART ONE
# **Business Leadership**

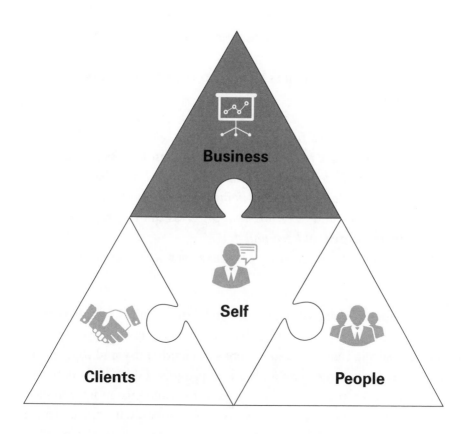

*Every new leader has an opportunity to inject energy and vision into their firm at the outset of their tenure. It is important to seize this moment by creating a sense of urgency, a burning platform, a compelling reason for changing the status quo.*
TIM DIXON-PHILLIP, CO-FOUNDER OF SERVICE REALITY, AND FORMER SALES AND MARKETING DIRECTOR AT EY

*Without a clear sense of vision firms lose their way. Yet vision alone is not enough: leaders who are very strong on strategy but very poor on delivery must surround themselves with able implementers in order to make their vision a reality.*
NICK HOLT, PARTNER AT SR SEARCH, AND FORMER MANAGING PARTNER AT KLEGAL

*The more complicated firms make their strategic plans, the less likely those plans are to be used in the way that they should be. The most able leaders recognize that strategic plans should be referred to on an almost daily basis, as a living and working tool to set goals and targets, and to ensure that progress can be properly and regularly monitored and evaluated.*
PHILIP GEORGE, FORMER MANAGING PARTNER AT BIRKETT LONG

Being a great leader of a professional firm requires effective business leadership. Traditionally, this meant keeping one eye on cash flows, ensuring that colleagues were sufficiently busy and that clients were billed regularly to avoid work in progress (WIP) becoming too high. However, professional services firms today are more complex businesses than ever before: they are more global, with more diverse operating models and operate in an ecosystem where the pace of change is incredibly fast. This complexity requires a new type of business leadership.

Though demand for professional services remains strong, and in many areas continues to increase, it is becoming harder for firms to make money simply by doing what they have always done. PricewaterhouseCooper's (PwC) annual study of the legal sector in the UK reveals that between 2010 and 2016 average profit margins for all but the top 10 UK law firms remained stagnant or had declined. Law firms in the 'squeezed middle' – those ranked 26 to 50 by turnover – have suffered most, with an average drop in margins from 27.2 per cent to 23.1 per cent. Across firms of all types and sizes, profit margin per chargeable hour has been on a downward trend over the last seven years (PwC, 2016).

As regulatory barriers to entry have broken down, competition in professional services has boomed. Competitors that look and operate very differently from the traditional pyramidal professional services firm have gained a foothold in the market over the last decade. Disruptors use technology or alternative resourcing models to meet client needs in totally new ways. Many of these new breeds of competitor have thrived; for example, Axiom, a provider of technology-enabled legal services, has grown on average 45 per cent each year since its inception in 2000 (Axiom, 2016). But it is not only the competitive landscape and new technologies that have fundamentally changed the way professional services firms operate as businesses. The nature of the advice they provide to clients and the kind of services they offer have evolved significantly as well.

Traditionally, clients had a problem and professionals advised: the decision, action and risk remained the clients' prerogative. Yet the rise of process-automation and self-service precedents has meant that it is more difficult for firms to make good money on their 'bread and butter' services. Profit margins are being slashed for all but the highest-value premium advice. Innovative professional services firms are exploring opportunities to turn a profit by having more skin in the game with their clients and taking responsibility for implementing their own advice in collaboration with clients. There may be more money to be made by the firms that take the risk of implementation away from their clients, but this requires a remodelling of the client-professional relationship and pricing structures that reflect this new way of working. The implication of these various business changes for leaders in professional services firms is profound. Leaders need to have a long-term vision for how they will respond to structural changes in the market while maintaining healthy levels of profitability. They also need to be more agile and opportunistic to take advantage of the faster pace of change. As a leader, how do you transform your firm and challenge the boundaries of the traditional professional services operating model? What kind of risk profile do you need to tolerate to retain competitive advantage, deepen client relationships and grow market share in light of disruptive competitors?

## Key questions considered in Business Leadership

In the three chapters in the Business Leadership section we will explore answers and case studies for the following questions:

In *Vision: how to create and implement a robust strategic plan* we answer:

- How do you create a strategy that will support long-term, sustainable profitability, and help you to maintain competitive advantage in your market?
- How can you develop a sense of shared purpose beyond financial success?
- How do you get buy-in to your strategy, within your firm, to ensure it is implemented effectively?

In *Innovation: how to reap the benefits of innovation in your firm* we consider:

- How can you create an entrepreneurial culture that tolerates risk and embraces innovation?
- How do you generate great ideas for new products, services and operating models?
- How do you successfully develop, scale and launch these new ideas?

In *Performance: how to improve the profitability of client engagements* we answer:

- How do you deal with price pressure from clients?
- How can you increase the profitability of your practice area or firm while maintaining employee and client satisfaction?
- How can small changes in financial management result in big gains in profitability?

# References

Axiom (2016) Axiom Law. Available from: www.axiomlaw.com [accessed 16 March 2017]

PwC (2016) *Annual Law Firms' Survey 2016*, PricewaterhouseCoopers. Available from: http://www.pwc.co.uk/industries/business-services/law-firms/survey.html [accessed 16 March 2017]

# Vision: how to create and implement a robust strategic plan

## 01

Jon Randall, COO at accountancy firm Moore Stephens, achieved his first leadership position when he was still in his thirties. He learnt that devising a strategy for professional services firms is a subtle skill that requires time and investment:

> To devise an effective strategy you have to listen more than you talk. Start with some fundamental questions: What markets do we want to break into? What clients do we want to work with? What kind of money do we want to make? Only when you have answered those questions does the work begin to persuade your staff and partners that your vision for the firm will deliver what they want. The simpler the picture of the strategy you can paint, the more consensus there will be that the firm is charting the right course to success.

Creating a strategy is one of the most important tasks for a newly appointed leader. A strategic review may occur once or twice in any leader's tenure but will often determine whether an individual's leadership is viewed as a success or failure by colleagues.

Most corporates have formal, well-established strategic planning processes. By contrast, professional services firms typically take a more ad hoc and less evidence-based approach to strategy development. Professionals will often be rigorous when solving their clients' issues but will take an informal approach to their own firm's strategy. Accountability for results and the rigorous review of progress against agreed targets are not often enforced within professional services firms. This holds back many firms from taking transformative decisions about their future strategic direction.

**Figure 1.1** The Bow Tie process

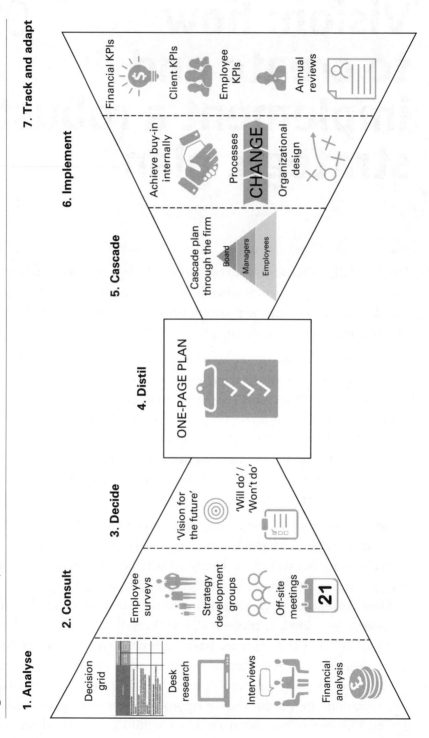

In our experience there is a simple seven step process that leaders can follow to develop, communicate and implement a strategic vision for their firm. We call this approach the Bow Tie process (see Figure 1.1). At its heart is a concise summary of the firm's strategic plan that all members of a firm can understand and buy into. This approach works equally well when developing a strategic plan for a team, department or sector group.

Our Bow Tie process is based on a few very simple principles. First, strategic planning is an evolving process that needs to be regularly reviewed and tweaked rather than a one-off exercise that quickly atrophies into irrelevance. Second, any strategy must be based on facts about a firm's clients and markets but overloading on information can lead to analysis paralysis. Third, engaging staff and partners in the process is crucial but leaders also need to make firm decisions and learn to say 'no' sometimes. And fourth, maintaining momentum by cascading and implementing the strategy through the firm is an often-overlooked driver of success.

# Step 1: analyse your clients and markets

All too often strategy in professional services firms is based solely on partner opinions, gut feelings or hunches, and not on the reality of clients and the market. Even the biggest professional services firms can fail to look upwards and outwards. The tendency for leaders is to look backwards and within for guidance. If a strategy is put together solely for internal reasons, to keep things ticking over, or is too risk-averse, it will fail to inspire and will not give sufficient impetus for change.

On the other hand, it is tempting to spend lots of time looking at data, forecasts and market reports trying to create a perfect plan. So how do you build the evidence base you need without becoming overwhelmed?

A helpful starting point is the 'Decision Grid', a framework we have used with numerous professional services firms – large and small – over the last two decades (see Figure 1.2). The decision grid is designed to be a discussion and planning tool for your senior leadership. It focuses minds on the strategic questions that need to be answered to create your strategic vision. It helps to get everybody aligned in one direction and defines the analysis needed to ensure fact-finding is tightly focused. The framework brings to the front of mind one fundamental question: will a given piece of analysis help to refine our strategy or not?

The first column of the decision grid contains your decisions. These are the high-level decisions that will determine your strategic vision. Start by agreeing which decisions need to be part of your strategy review: is a root and branch refresh of your firm's strategic options necessary, or do you want to focus on a particular area such as Business Development (BD) strategy or operations? It may be helpful to think about grouping the decisions in the three areas of the Leadership Triangle: clients, business and people.

The second column contains initial hypotheses against each of the decisions. It is helpful to start by capturing what you and your colleagues believe are the right answers. Within your firm there will be a huge amount of existing knowledge and getting this on the table at the outset will prevent you from spending time collecting fresh evidence on points where good data already exists. The hypothesis capture will also reveal where opinions differ. The fact-find and analysis should then focus on contentious areas to provide solid evidence that cannot be questioned later.

The third column contains fact-find questions. These are the specific questions you need to investigate to provide evidence to support your strategic decisions. For example, if a strategic decision is 'What markets and clients do we want to serve?' then you will want to explore questions about the current profitability of different client segments, the intensity of competition and which market sectors are anticipated to grow strongly.

In the final column you should summarize the headlines from your fact-find in response to your fact-find questions. In some instances evidence will emerge to support initial hypotheses; in other instances the fact-find will provide new evidence that challenges or adds nuances to initial thinking. Using these results you can then begin to agree answers to the decisions in the first column.

In our experience there are various ways to carry out the fact-find stage to build the evidence base you need to inform your strategic decisions. A mix of sources and research methods will help to build a comprehensive picture of the strategic opportunities for your firm.

**Figure 1.2**    An example of a decision grid

| | 1. DECISIONS | 2. HYPOTHESES | 3. QUESTIONS THE ANALYSIS NEEDS TO ANSWER | 4. FINDINGS FROM THE ANALYSIS |
|---|---|---|---|---|
| **CLIENTS** | What markets and clients do we want to serve (existing and new)? | | • Which clients are most profitable?<br>• Which segments have greatest growth potential?<br>• Where are we facing the most competition? | |
| | What services will we provide (existing and new)? | | • Which services are most profitable?<br>• Which services have greatest growth potential? | |
| **BUSINESS** | What is our value proposition? How do we create value for clients and differentiate from the competition? | | • What are the client benefits of our services?<br>• How do these benefits translate into bottom-line benefits?<br>• How is our approach different from our competitors? | |
| | How do we ensure that the firm's operations are aligned to deliver our value proposition? | | • How do we need to change our structure and processes to help us compete (IT, marketing, HR, finance)? | |
| | How do we create a profitable economic model? | | • What revenues can we expect?<br>• What profits will be delivered?<br>• What PEP/dividends are expected?<br>• What is our target level of overheads and variable costs?<br>• What investment will be required? | |
| **PEOPLE** | How do we create an environment that attracts the best talent and enables them to perform at their peak? | | • What is our recruitment policy?<br>• What is our reward and performance management approach?<br>• How will we hone our people's skills? | |

We recommend starting with desk research. There is a huge amount of publicly available information that will help you to map out industry trends and understand what competitors are doing. Useful sources include industry reports, directories, financial benchmarks and league tables, competitor websites, analyst reports and press reports. Desk research alone, however, is usually not sufficient to answer all your fact-find questions.

Talking to the market can provide valuable answers. As a leader it is beneficial to spend plenty of time meeting clients, intermediaries and market experts to build up a picture of the markets in which you operate. One leader in a global law firm describes how the process of gathering client insight works in her firm:

> Our Chairman regularly has private meetings with our most senior clients to talk about the relationship, what is important to them and what is happening in their different sectors. These conversations are an opportunity to discuss issues that are at the top of our clients' minds, reveal how their needs are changing and often identify needs that are currently unmet by us and our competitors. This market intelligence is then fed back into the firm and we draw on this kind of insight during our formal strategy planning cycle.

As well as the informal approach, a structured programme of client interviews can add tremendous insight and provide more definite answers to the fact-finding questions in the decision grid. Depending on the complexity of the questions you seek to answer – and whether you are looking for statistics, qualitative insights or both – this information can be gained through in-depth interviews or through a telephone or online survey.

Mark House, a former executive director at wealth advisers Coutts, summarizes the benefits of client research:

> An awful lot of business decisions are made on the basis of unchallenged facts. In our industry disruption is always around the corner, and the more information you can get about that, the more fresh and relevant insight about your clients you can collect, the better informed the strategic decisions you take will be. In my experience the only way firms can do that is to ask questions of their clients, listen and then act.

However, carrying out client interviews is a skill and to get the most value from the conversations requires proper planning. Drafting a discussion guide of themes and questions gives structure to the conversation. We recommend adopting a discussion guide structure similar to that outlined in Figure 1.3, which leads the conversation from more general observations about a client's business and market to more specific implications and the next steps for the firm.

**Figure 1.3**   An example of an interview discussion guide flow

What are the issues facing the clients at a personal and organizational level?

What trends in the market will influence how the client uses external advisers? Where will external spend likely increase or decrease?

How does the client view your firm and its service quality, brand and specialisms? How does it view your value proposition?

How does the client view your competitors? What can your firm learn from them?

What are the best opportunities for your firm to grow share of wallet?

What does your firm need to do to unlock more fees and deepen the relationship with clients?

Next steps

During the recession of the late 2000s and early 2010s, well-run professional services firms got their cost base, leverage structure and cash management under control. However, to make strategic decisions about future investments or priorities, it is essential to know where you make and spend money and from which areas of the business your profits come.

Ask your finance department to slice and dice existing financial data to find out which offices, clients and practice groups are driving revenue and gross margin. Take this baseline and then predict which segments and services are likely to grow in the next three years and which will decline. Star performers meet three criteria: high revenue generation, high profit margin and high growth potential.

Having reliable management information can provide invaluable answers to your fact-finding questions. The more granular the data the better, as it will enable you to attribute a realistic proportion of the overall cost of running your firm to each fee-earner, so that you can assess the profit generated by that person and their team. Once you know the relevant cost assumptions you can aggregate at office, sector or practice-group level and use this insight to inform decisions about where to direct marketing spend and other budget items.

## Step 2: consult with internal stakeholders

Creating a strategy is not a top-down exercise. In consensus-driven and collegiate environments like professional services firms, all individuals need to feel some involvement in the strategic vision of the firm in order to get on board with the changes that will result from the strategy. Increasingly, leaders actively ask people in their firm for input and feedback on the firm's strategic direction. Staff at all levels – partners, business services staff and other fee-earners – have a valuable contribution to offer and are often closer to the market than senior management.

The process of involving staff in strategy creation keeps them involved and engaged. There is a range of useful tools to gather staff views, including:

- employee surveys and online polls;
- online collaboration tools, discussion boards and forums;

- strategy development groups with representatives from different parts of the firm;

- structured one-on-one or small group consultation conversations with internal colleagues; and

- firm-wide or team workshops and off-site events.

The conference or off-site event is an excellent opportunity to consult and get buy-in to a new strategic direction but in our view is one of the major missed opportunities in many professional services firms. The stakes can be high: managed poorly and the off-site occasion will be nothing more than a 'talking shop' with animated discussion of issues and half-formed ideas but no overall consensus or conclusions. At the other extreme, attendees may feel they are being presented with a fait accompli and are being railroaded into a strategy about which they have not been properly consulted.

Of the many professional services firm conferences we have been involved in over the last two decades, the most successful follow the broad five-step approach outlined below:

1 **Pre-reading:** prior to the conference, analysis and information is shared with attendees in a succinct form, ideally including a one-page summary or infographic. In the pre-read material highlight the decisions that the conference will be used to inform, the options for consideration, and where attendees can find more detailed analysis should they wish to do further reading.

2 **Presentation:** during the conference itself, present the analysis, leaving plenty of time for Q&A so attendees can feel comfortable that the analysis presented is robust. It is important to build a broad consensus on where your firm sits in the market today, and the opportunities and challenges facing the firm. If there is fundamental disagreement on where the firm is now it is very hard to build agreement on how it should develop in the future.

3 **Breakout groups and consultations:** split attendees into breakout groups, ideally not more than 10 people per group. Provide worksheets and very clear instructions of what you would like people to discuss; also how you would like people to record information and present this back later on. The breakout process should encourage

creativity and a positive mindset. External facilitation can really help and it can also be valuable to take people out of the office so that distractions are minimized.

4 **Plenary session**: few conferences leave adequate time for a proper plenary. This is an opportunity for the whole group to come back together to consider the implications of the breakout conversations and to hear from a wider selection of colleagues. Ask nominated spokespeople to present back from each breakout group, and allow plenty of time for discussion and to agree the main principles. In some instances it may be beneficial to take a vote or show-of-hands on these core strategic principles to demonstrate the collective buy-in to the decisions.

5 **Follow-up**: momentum is often lost after an off-site event. To avoid this, ask a nominated person to promptly write up notes of the ideas generated and circulate a copy to all attendees with agreed next steps, including the accountable person and the delivery date for any actions. The follow-up is also a useful opportunity to collect further ideas or to take a poll on the best ideas emerging from the off-site event to take forwards.

## Step 3: decide on your priorities

There is a time for consultation and a time for making decisions. As a leader you have to decide upon a vision for the future that is in tune with the partnership's appetite for change. It is okay for this vision to be two steps ahead of the partnership but not 10 steps.

Historically, the strategic vision for professional services firms focused on financial targets or geographic expansion. However, in the last decade a more balanced vision has emerged in many firms that incorporates elements of people and clients. Nick Holt, former managing partner of KLegal and now a partner of SR Search, a specialist legal recruitment firm, has witnessed this change from a narrow focus on financials to a broader sense of purpose and vision:

> Successful firms build their strategy and vision around happy people and happy clients. Firms that sweat their resources too hard will find their people won't be happy and this will result in them not serving

their clients very well. A vision, therefore, has to be positive and future-looking. It has to give people a reason to continue doing what they love to do and to show them how their contribution will be beneficial to clients and to the firm's financial success.

A good way for a leader to frame this vision for the future is to decide how the firm will change over the next three years, and then describe the impact on the three elements of the Leadership Triangle. For example:

- Business: what will success look like from a business perspective in terms of growth, revenues, market profile or profits?
- Clients: how will we add value to our clients? Which types of clients will we serve, what is our differentiator and how will we enhance our client experience?
- People: how will we create a great environment for our people? What sort of work–life balance do we want to achieve? How will we enhance people's skills and how will we provide interesting work?

Where leaders often come unstuck is in their reluctance to say 'no'. It is relatively easy to identify possible new initiatives or client segments but much more difficult to decide which offices, practice areas or sectors you will exit. The temptation to agree to all ideas is strong as you want to keep everybody in the firm happy. However, an inability to prioritize and take difficult decisions can lead to a dilution of focus and long-term underperformance.

Faced with difficult decisions, some leaders defer them in the hope that they will go away or will be resolved thanks to unforeseen circumstances. In reality most problems, if not immediately tackled, get much bigger. Philip George, the former managing partner of East Anglian law firm Birkett Long, outlines one example where a difficult strategic choice taken during his leadership was turned into a positive outcome:

Our Halstead office had existed for nearly 200 years and continued to contribute to the firm's overall profitability. However, we were finding it increasingly difficult to recruit young lawyers to it: our bright youngsters preferred to work in the larger commercial centres in Colchester and Chelmsford. The problem was such a large one, it was tempting to procrastinate but we recognized that there was an opportunity to be grasped instead. Our much newer Chelmsford office had been opened as a commercial office only but it very quickly became evident that there was a demand for private client services there also. We therefore decided to solve the issue on our own terms by closing the Halstead office and transferring most of the personnel to Chelmsford, rather than manage a steady decline in profitability from the Halstead office.

**CASE STUDY** Arup: a firm with a strategy and purpose

Arup is an independent firm of designers, planners, engineers, consultants and technical specialists offering a broad range of professional services for all aspects of the built environment. Founded in 1946 by Sir Ove Arup, with an initial focus on structural engineering, Arup first came to the world's attention with the structural design of the Sydney Opera House, followed by its work on the Pompidou Centre in Paris. Although UK domiciled, it is an international firm with a presence in many countries and an international mindset.

Over his tenure in the eponymous organization Sir Ove Arup developed what was to become the firm's core values and priorities, captured in a speech he gave to partners in 1970 known as the Key Speech. Some 70 years after the founding of the firm the tenets of the Key Speech remain to this day at the core of its identity. The values state:

- We will ensure that the Arup name is always associated with quality.
- We will act honestly and fairly in dealings with our staff and others.
- We will enhance prosperity for all Arup staff.

Underpinning these core values Arup identified six core aims of the firm. These are:

- quality of work;
- total architecture;
- humane organization;
- straight and honourable dealings;
- social usefulness;
- reasonable prosperity of members.

The fact that the Key Speech has remained at the core of today's firm comes from a small number of fine balances that Arup – perhaps due to his background in philosophy as well as engineering – was able to navigate.

*Tolerance of conflicts and tensions*

He accepted that there were tensions and conflicts between the various aims; for example, between the aim of 'quality of work' and the aim of a 'reasonable prosperity of members'. In accepting these imperfections, he identified that there was a need to balance the relative priorities of each of them to create success.

*Pull versus push*

In his own words Arup 'disliked hard principles, ideologies and the like' and therefore accepted that the aims should not be imposed on, but sold to the members of the firm. 'I would like to persuade them that these are good and reasonable and not too impossible, aims possessing an inner cohesion, reinforcing each other by being not only aims but means to each others' fulfilment' he said.

*Flexibility and adaptability*

Linked to the concept of pull rather than push, he accepted that the aims needed to be flexible and adaptable. Temporary diversions from them were acceptable, or inevitable, but what was important was that after such a temporary diversion they would always get back on course.

*Common purpose*

The fourth and, arguably the most important insight, was that the purpose of the aims was to articulate what binds the firm together. 'I can't see the point in having such a large firm with offices all over the world unless there is something that binds us together. If we were just ordinary consulting engineers carrying on business just as business to make a comfortable living, I can't see why each office couldn't carry on, on its own.'

As Arup approaches 70 years as a company, and nearly 30 years after Ove Arup died, there is currently significant focus within the organization on revisiting their aims and looking at what they mean in today's world. This adaptability is a real strength of the way Ove chose to articulate his guidance for future generations.

# Step 4: distil your strategy into its fundamental principles

After having spent time and effort developing a strategy, there is a danger that many leaders in professional services firms communicate the strategy to only a handful of senior individuals and not to the people within the firm who will actually be expected to implement many of the components of the strategy. In too many firms a really well-thought-through strategy is unfortunately put in a drawer and forgotten about rather than used as an ongoing management tool.

To avoid these pitfalls, we recommend condensing the strategy into a very short plan limited to a page or two that can be shared with staff. Some firms even share this summary with clients or use it on

**Figure 1.4**    An example of a one-page strategy plan

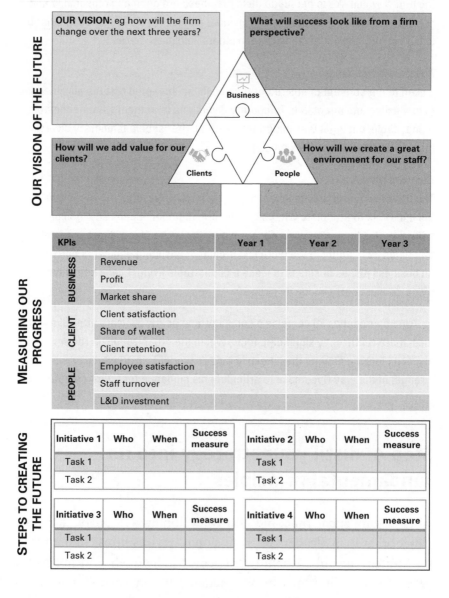

their website, in pitches or other marketing materials. If your strategy cannot be reduced to a page or two, then it is almost certainly too complicated for others in the firm to understand and the chances of successful implementation are low.

Robert Duggan is the managing partner of the London office of offshore law firm Mourant Ozannes. When creating a strategy for his firm, he condensed down the key points into a one-page infographic:

> In my experience the best business plans are succinct. To help commu-
> nicate the key strands of our business plan to colleagues I scaled
> everything down to a one-page document that describes what our
> practice is and the types of work we do. The information is represented
> simply and visually. My aim was that any of my partners should be
> able to understand the strategy in five minutes. We spent time creating a
> narrative for Mourant Ozannes and we wanted to retain that clarity of
> thought when communicating the firm's strategy.

An example of a one-page plan is provided opposite (see Figure 1.4). Its brevity means that it forces clarity of thinking and, because it is easy to understand, it is more likely to guide the behaviour of staff towards desired outcomes. A typical distillation of a strategy into a single page would include a summary of the overall vision, head-line KPIs (key performance indicators) that you will use to measure and track success against the vision, and a high-level description of no more than a handful of key initiatives or programmes that will underpin the implementation of the strategy.

## Step 5: cascade the strategy throughout the firm

Just as it is important to communicate your strategic vision to colleagues, any strategic plan needs to be cascaded throughout the firm to help people understand what the strategy means for them in practice: what are they expected to do differently and why? One of the most common reasons for the failure of a strategy within professional services firms is that, although people acknowledge the credibility of a firm-wide vision or goal, they silently opt out of the strategy when it comes to changing the way that they or their team work.

A successful approach is to cascade the firm-wide strategic plan into a series of separate but integrated plans owned by different teams or departments, or to identify firm-wide initiatives or work-streams arising out of the strategy, as illustrated in Figure 1.5. For example, the firm-wide business plan should be underpinned by individual team plans, which should be regularly reviewed at team meetings. This will help people to understand what they need to do to make a relevant contribution to furthering the success of the firm-wide strategic vision. More details about cascading strategy into personal development plans can be found in the People section of this handbook.

To be effective, any team plan or workstream plan also needs to have clear, realistic goals, KPIs and actions that will bring about the desired strategic change. In some instances it will be appropriate for these KPIs and actions to be taken directly from the firm-wide strategy, while in other instances KPIs may need to be adjusted to account for the types of work undertaken by different teams. For example, a profit margin KPI may be different for audit and tax teams in an accountancy firm, but client satisfaction metrics may be consistent across all service line strategies.

**Figure 1.5**   Cascading a one-page plan throughout the organization

# Step 6: implement your strategy within the team

Most strategy reviews give rise to change but leading change can be tough. Often leaders underestimate the difficulty of changing how people think, act and behave. Conversely, they often overestimate their firm's capabilities and its capacity for change.

As a leader you have to find an appropriate balance between aspiration and reality. Too mundane and unambitious and a strategy will fail to inspire confidence in your leadership; too overambitious and the overwhelming, unrealistic nature of the task at hand can quickly demoralize many people.

In our experience people within professional services firms only accept change and take action to implement that change if they believe three criteria have been met:

1 **They see the value of the change to themselves** – ie they expect to benefit personally in some way by agreeing to change. Although this perceived benefit might be financial, in many cases professionals are motivated by non-financial factors such as the quality of client work, an enhanced personal reputation in the market and an improved work–life balance.

2 **They believe that the change can and will be delivered successfully** – ie they see the leadership in their firm as credible and capable of following through on their strategic vision. Professionals typically will only pull their weight if they believe the leadership has set the right direction and that colleagues who actively undermine change efforts will be admonished for doing so.

3 **They understand their individual role in achieving that change** – ie they feel capable and empowered to make a contribution to the change effort. As outlined above, people need to be able to make a clear link in their minds between the principal strategic vision and their own personal or team plan.

In most cases it is sensible for implementation to occur incrementally so that the firm is not overwhelmed by trying to implement too much change simultaneously. In our experience most strategic reviews flag up opportunities to make changes to a range of areas for the firm: from business development and marketing plans, brand messages and key client management, through to skills and training, systems, processes and management information.

Each of these changes will require time and investment, and in many cases will be interdependent, so it is important to plan carefully and prioritize effort where possible. In order not to get overwhelmed you may find it useful to use the following checklist of questions to determine whether any proposed strategic change is a sensible investment for your firm:

- Will the new way of doing things be meaningfully and measurably better than what we have done to date?

- Is the plan realistic, given past experience and our firm's capabilities? Do we need to make additional investment in people or systems before we can embark on the required change?

- Who really benefits from this change and why? Is it just personal posturing, or will it allow us to serve clients better and/or more profitably?

- Does the person driving the change have the political capital and determination to see it through?

- Are we 'all changed out' or can we cope, collectively, with doing more?

- Can we make changes in stages and can we adjust our course as we go along if need be?

- What would our clients and our staff say about us before and what do we want them to say about us after the change?

- How can we minimize the disruption to staff during the change process to ensure that their experience is as positive as possible?

## Step 7: track and adapt progress against your strategy

As a leader how do you know if your strategic vision is on track? A good set of KPIs should act as your compass, helping you and your team to understand whether you're taking the right path towards your strategic goals and where you are falling behind.

One leading accountancy firm, for example, has enunciated 10 measurable goals (known colloquially as the 'Power of Ten') to help guide the firm towards its vision of becoming the leading provider of audit and advisory services for mid-market clients and to support a demanding revenue-growth target. The strategic goals are non-financial and cover measurable improvements in areas such as quality, client service, brand awareness, sector expertise and market segment pre-eminence in chosen areas.

However, it can be tempting to max yourself out on too many KPIs. Each measurement is likely to require its own set of processes to calculate and report, so each new measurement creates an additional time burden on your teams that may take time away from higher value tasks. In our view, the most effective KPIs must:

- be well-defined and quantifiable;

- link back to your strategic goals;

- be relatively easy to generate, and if possible a by-product of 'business as usual';

- be communicated throughout your organization;

- contribute towards ongoing decision-making; and

- be cascaded and customized for each team, where appropriate.

The typical approach executive teams use to cascade their strategic KPIs is to produce a clear set of firm-wide goals and for each department or leader to take this on board and customize it for their part of the firm. Ideally, KPIs should be reflected in staff appraisals and more information about this is included later in this handbook.

Although leaders should not change their strategy year-on-year, it is important to monitor and formally review the strategy at least once a year to assess whether targets and milestones are being reached and where a change in direction may be required. In our experience the most effective leaders always keep one eye on the changing world beyond their firm to understand how the economic cycle, regulatory change or the emergence of new competitors may influence the strategic direction the firm is headed in.

**SUMMARY** Top tips for creating a vision and
implementing a strategy

### Build a robust evidence base for decisions to gain internal buy-in for your vision

Spend sufficient time gathering facts about your clients and markets, ideally by talking to clients directly about their needs and experiences. Professional market research can provide extremely valuable insight. Understand where your firm currently makes money and which types of clients, work and departments are profitable now and how that might change over the economic cycle. But avoid analysis paralysis: there will be a time when additional analysis will muddy the waters rather than make things clearer.

### Involve as many people internally as possible to create a shared sense of vision

Staff surveys and workshops are invaluable tools for gathering views on strategic direction. They also send a powerful signal that you, as a leader, are open to consultation and taking guidance from others. Find areas of consensus to build a shared sense of purpose. Financial targets are just one of many motivators for professionals. Happy staff deliver great service; great service results in recurring revenue.

### Don't avoid tough decisions

If your leadership tenure is time-limited it can be tempting to keep the tiller steady until it is time to hand over to the next person. In reality, doing nothing is an effective strategy for very few professional firms: as the market evolves so should your firm. An effective strategy is about deciding which opportunities to pursue and when to say 'no'. Weak leaders lack focus, which usually results in a dilution of potential success.

### Communicate frequently to make your vision as real for people as possible

Busy professionals have little time to read long strategy papers but will make time to digest and think about a strategy that has been distilled down to a page or two. Communicate frequently and use formal and informal channels to get your message across: email, face-to-face and group meetings. Help people to understand what you want them to do differently and the outcomes you expect to achieve.

**Maintain momentum after launch by regularly reviewing performance**

Successful strategies are about much more than big bang launches. Develop a handful of meaningful performance indicators that will enable you to track progress and regularly share updates with colleagues to motivate and inspire progress. Regular light-touch reviews will enable you to identify underperformers early who might need additional time and attention to help them get back on track.

# Innovation: how to reap the benefits of innovation in your firm

## 02

In 2011, IBM's artificial intelligence (AI) software Watson won an exhibition match of the American quiz show *Jeopardy!* against past champions Brad Rutter and Ken Jennings. Not only did Watson beat two of the show's most successful human contestants, it did so convincingly by amassing a prize pot more than three times bigger than either Rutter or Jennings (Best, 2013).

Watson uses cognitive computing to learn from its mistakes: it gets smarter over time as more data is fed into it and it can begin to anticipate or predict patterns of information and behaviour. IBM's Watson technology is being used in a range of industries, from healthcare and weather forecasting to professional services. IBM has now licensed Watson to other firms to develop their own services using its artificial brainpower.

Within a very short space of time AI and automation technology has gained a strong foothold in the professional services sector. As an example, in the UK, ThoughtRiver provides a contract risk evaluation tool and dashboard based on AI technology. Building on IBM Watson technology, the Toronto-based ROSS Intelligence has developed software to speed up legal research. A user can ask questions in plain English and ROSS will then search through the entire body of law to return an answer based on its reading of relevant legislation, case law and other secondary sources.

The technology is spreading and into all areas of professional services, not just law. We are at the outset of a wave of innovation that will potentially change the way professionals spend their time and the value they deliver to clients. If much of what a professional spends their time doing can be automated, or delivered by lesser-qualified professionals such as paralegals or accounting technicians, often based offshore, is this good news or bad news for the traditional professional firm? Will it make professionals irrelevant, or will it free up their time to focus on high value advice?

Successful professional services leaders don't fear innovation, they embrace it. However, innovation cannot be left to chance: finding, refining and launching good ideas requires leadership and process. This chapter provides a guide to innovation in professional services. It will help you to understand how traditional professional firms have responded to the threat of disruptors shaking up their market with radically simpler and cheaper services using technology and new delivery models. We show that, to thrive in the future professional services firms need to take a more strategic approach to innovation, and that there are simple lessons that can help any leader to adopt more successful innovation practices in their firm, regardless of its size.

# The six ages of innovation

Some industry commentators would have you believe that professional services firms are slow-moving dinosaurs, extremely vulnerable to more agile start-ups. There is undoubtedly an element of truth in this: lawyers and accountants are trained to focus on risk not opportunity, and those professionals are at the helm of the majority of the leading professional firms. The partnership structure itself also makes agile decision-making hard.

However, on closer examination, the argument that professional services firms are incapable of innovation is wrong. Roll back 10, 20 or 30 years and you will find a professional services landscape that looks very different from today. Since the 1980s the professions have shown an immense ability to adapt and change. Their path of continued innovation is charted in the six ages of innovation in Figure 2.1

**Figure 2.1** The six ages of innovation

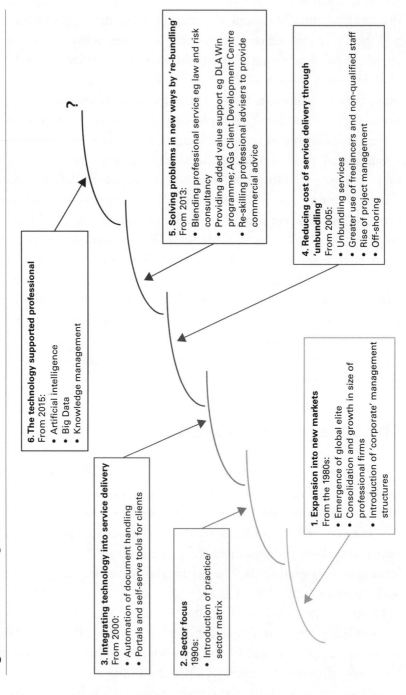

**6. The technology supported professional**
From 2015:
- Artificial intelligence
- Big Data
- Knowledge management

**5. Solving problems in new ways by 're-bundling'**
From 2013:
- Blending professional service eg law and risk consultancy
- Providing added value support eg DLA Win programme; AGs Client Development Centre
- Re-skilling professional advisers to provide commercial advice

**4. Reducing cost of service delivery through 'unbundling'**
From 2005:
- Unbundling services
- Greater use of freelancers and non-qualified staff
- Rise of project management
- Off-shoring

**3. Integrating technology into service delivery**
From 2000:
- Automation of document handling
- Portals and self-serve tools for clients

**2. Sector focus**
1990s:
- Introduction of practice/sector matrix

**1. Expansion into new markets**
From the 1980s:
- Emergence of global elite
- Consolidation and growth in size of professional firms
- Introduction of 'corporate' management structures

?

Through this process of continued evolution, professional services has become one of the most successful and powerful industry sectors in many Western economies.

## Age one – expansion into new markets

In little over 30 years the leading professional firms have grown from cottage industries to global, multimillion-pound businesses. Market deregulation allowed growth and internationalism in a way that had not been possible before. The use of the Swiss Verein structure allowed more international collaborations and the arrival of the LLP in the early 2000s gave a further boost by allowing partners to control their exposure to risk to a greater degree.

As firms grew in size and developed more diverse services for their clients, they adopted governance structures with a stronger corporate flavour. This provided greater management oversight to ensure greater consistency and better financial management.

## Age two – sector focus

The next innovation wave was the development of the matrix structure that married together technical disciplines with a focus on industry sectors. This created a change in the way that professionals took their expertise to clients, including physically sitting together in sector groups.

## Age three – integrating technology into service delivery

The fourth wave of innovation occurred around the mid-2000s when technology became much better integrated into service delivery. Firms began to use technology to speed up and automate the sifting and management of large amounts of documents and data. Electronic deal rooms and client portals are now the norm, and project management software gives clients greater visibility of the progress of work.

## Age four – reducing cost of service delivery through 'un-bundling'

The global financial crisis was the catalyst for more change. As clients became increasingly cost-conscious, firms looked for ways to cut the cost of service delivery. Most tightened up on their project management and pricing. Others took more radical steps such as off-shoring routine work to low cost centres and making use of different types of resource such as freelancers and non-qualified staff. They 'un-bundled' typical client processes such as an M&A deal to work out the best resourcing model for each component part. Although some firms feared these innovations would be seen as commoditizing the traditional work of professionals, they actually helped to deliver better outcomes for clients without damaging brand value.

## Age five – solving problems in new ways through 're-bundling'

Another tipping point was reached in the early 2010s. Firms leading this wave of innovation realized that to maintain margins they had to devise ways of providing smarter, not just cheaper, solutions for their clients. We refer to this as 're-bundling' because it involves combining different disciplines and business models into an integrated, holistic service. Examples of this wave of innovation include law firms offering consultancy advice, and management consultancy firms blending consultancy with data analytics and artificial intelligence.

## Age six – the technology-supported professional

We are now entering a new wave of innovation: the technology-supported professional. In this new age technology and innovation are bringing about fundamental changes in how professionals work and the tasks they undertake. Technology will not just speed up work, but will mean professionals work in completely new ways.

Many professionals recognize that the market has changed. Altman Weil, a US-based consultancy, has undertaken research with managing partners at US law firms, asking whether various trends are temporary or permanent. At least 83 per cent of the managing partners surveyed believed that competition from non-traditional providers is a permanent trend. Nearly three-quarters (73 per cent) believe that the pace of change in the professions will increase (Altman Weil, 2016).

It seems clear that one result of this wave of innovation is a more complex professional services ecosystem. Different types of competitors have already emerged to challenge the dominance of incumbents. Professional services solutions are being delivered by technology businesses, publishers, start-ups, retailers and in-house departments at large corporates. Here are just three examples of successful disruptors from a variety of professional disciplines:

- Narrative Science, founded in 2010, has an artificial intelligence system, Quill, that analyses raw data and generates reports in seconds. Its use of natural language processing produces outputs that readers would assume were written by a human author. This work would historically have been undertaken by consultancy firms.

- Crunch, founded in 2008, provides self-service online accountancy services to SMEs for a much lower price than high street accountancy firms.

- Eden McCullum, founded in 2000, works with experienced, freelance consultants to deliver high-end consulting engagements for its clients. Its delivery model draws in alumni from Bain, BCG and McKinsey to deliver premium quality work at a fraction of the cost of traditional competitors.

The disruptors are not simply reducing the cost of delivery, they are also delivering a simpler, more consistent client experience. Their impact should not be underestimated: they are both taking market share and recalibrating what clients come to expect from their professional advisers. As a leader your colleagues will look to you for leadership and direction on these difficult strategic issues: you need to understand how innovation will affect your firm and how to tweak your strategy to grasp the innovation opportunities and avoid the threats.

# Incumbents are well-placed to thrive, if they embrace innovation

Many professional services firms have embraced innovation and have been very successful in doing so. The Big Four accounting firms, for example, have transformed over the last quarter century from predominantly being audit practices to firms combining accounting, tax, deals and consulting capabilities. As they have innovated, the Big Four firms have had to change their delivery model; for example, by developing online accounting and tax services and moving resources into lower-cost centres. That has enabled them to compete successfully in more price-sensitive markets where the Big Four would have been seen as too expensive just five or ten years ago.

Allen & Overy is another example of a firm that has benefited strongly from a focus on business model innovation. The firm recognized that market and client demands were changing and that they were on the cusp of what the firm's then-senior partner David Morley called in 2014 'arguably the biggest revolution in legal services in the last 200 years' (Allen & Overy, 2014).

This focus on innovation didn't happen by accident. Allen & Overy took a systematic approach to planning their innovation strategy. They undertook a series of structured conversations with nearly 200 of their clients across 27 countries with the help of consultancy Meridian West. Clients were asked about their legal needs and their appetite for using different types of legal services. A clear consensus emerged: clients were open to using the firm for non-traditional services, and were particularly attracted to a one-stop-shop solution but only if Allen & Overy could guarantee a high quality service. Rather than see the firm as moving 'downmarket' by embracing new delivery models, the vast majority of clients said it would be a brand-enhancing strategy for Allen & Overy.

Using the insights from their client research, Allen & Overy developed a range of non-traditional legal services for its clients. It was one of the first major law firms to embrace a complementary suite of delivery models. These include Peerpoint (which provides clients with access to experienced, high-calibre lawyers who work flexibly on contract), online subscription products to help reduce legal, regulatory and operational risk, and a Legal Services Centre (LSC) based in Belfast. The LSC is led by an experienced partner and staffed by junior legal professionals who handle routine transaction-related work including document reviews, drafting and research tasks.

These two examples show that even successful firms at the top of their respective markets recognize the need to innovate. In each case, rather than lose market share to disruptive competitors, the firms have embraced delivery innovation to meet client expectations and secure future revenue streams.

# The innovation lifecycle: make the innovation process work better for your firm

As a leader it is not out of your reach to replicate the success of firms such as Allen & Overy, regardless of your firm's size or innovation track record. In our experience there are simple rules and approaches that work for professional services firms to develop a strategy for incubating and launching innovative products and services. We call these rules and approaches the Innovation Lifecycle (see Figure 2.2). The lifecycle is divided into five sequential phases, plus a strategic phase – Phase 0 – that provide the necessary architecture and infrastructure upon which to build successful innovation.

## *Phase zero – innovation strategy formulation*

Before starting any innovation project, it is crucial to plan your approach. You need to think through how your approach to innovation links with your overall strategic vision, as articulated in the previous chapter. This means getting the right balance of incremental and radical innovation, and putting in place the appropriate financial and people resources to sustain any innovation project. Before you begin, ask yourself: what are the real-world capabilities of your current people, systems and infrastructure? How far can they be stretched to achieve the innovation outcome you are looking for?

**Figure 2.2** The innovation lifecycle

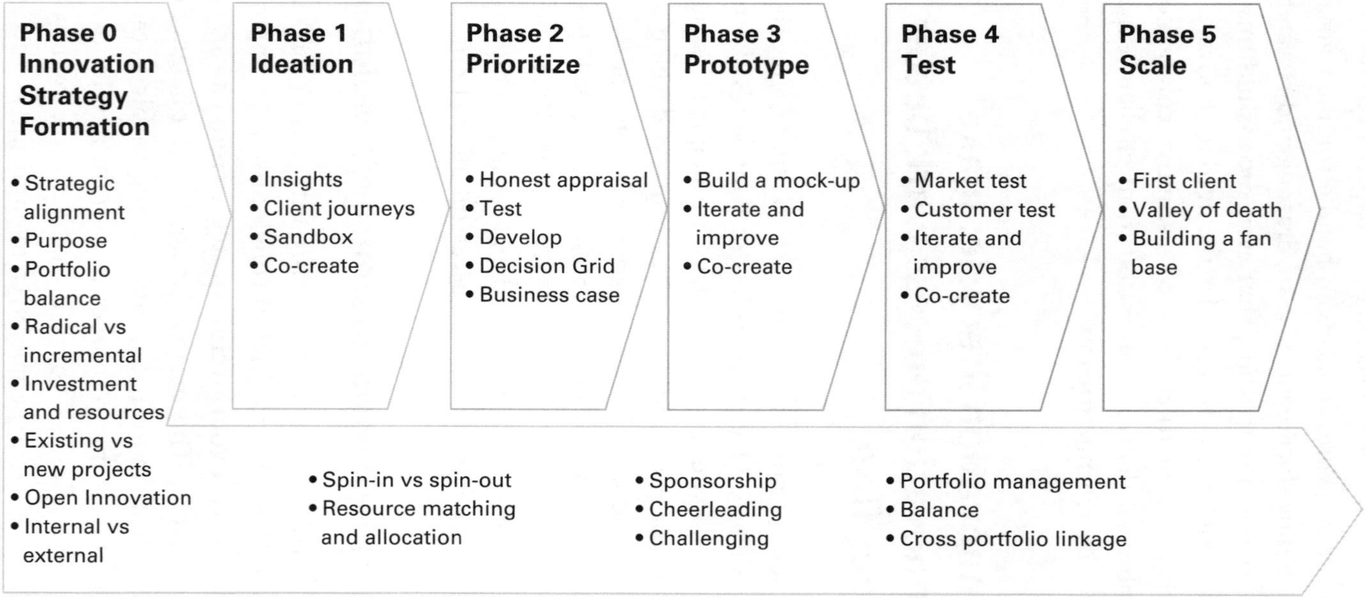

| Phase 0 Innovation Strategy Formation | Phase 1 Ideation | Phase 2 Prioritize | Phase 3 Prototype | Phase 4 Test | Phase 5 Scale |
|---|---|---|---|---|---|
| • Strategic alignment<br>• Purpose<br>• Portfolio balance<br>• Radical vs incremental<br>• Investment and resources<br>• Existing vs new projects<br>• Open Innovation<br>• Internal vs external | • Insights<br>• Client journeys<br>• Sandbox<br>• Co-create | • Honest appraisal<br>• Test<br>• Develop<br>• Decision Grid<br>• Business case | • Build a mock-up<br>• Iterate and improve<br>• Co-create | • Market test<br>• Customer test<br>• Iterate and improve<br>• Co-create | • First client<br>• Valley of death<br>• Building a fan base |
| | • Spin-in vs spin-out<br>• Resource matching and allocation | | • Sponsorship<br>• Cheerleading<br>• Challenging | • Portfolio management<br>• Balance<br>• Cross portfolio linkage | |

When people discuss innovation they tend to think of radically new products and services. However, leaders should have a strategy for both incremental innovation and radical innovation. Incremental innovation could be focused on improving efficiency through case management software, improving account management, or fine-tuning the way you serve clients.

More radical innovations, on the other hand, could include developing online services, embracing artificial intelligence, or creating completely new propositions such as offering clients contract professionals or developing new consultancy services.

Getting the right balance between the two groups of innovation is vitally important. If you back too many radical innovations there is a danger that time and resources are poured into initiatives that may not work while the core business is neglected. Conversely, many professional services firms are too conservative. There is a real risk that the market shifts and their competitors move ahead.

It is helpful to think in terms of managing a portfolio of innovations and to prioritize accordingly. Innovations that have the potential to have a big impact but require little investment in time and money are clearly priorities. High investment but low impact ideas should be nipped in the bud, now. High investment but high impact ideas need to be scrutinized and market-tested early to validate the business case before pouring in money and time.

As a leader you need to be honest with yourself and avoid the common pitfall of backing pet projects that live too long and have no justifiable business case. Here are some questions to ask yourself when setting your innovation strategy to avoid falling into this trap:

- Is there a correct balance in our portfolio between radical and incremental innovation?
- Are we organised in the right way to make innovation happen?
- Do we have the right culture and environment to foster innovation and access to appropriate resources and people?
- Do we appraise innovation efforts honestly?
- Do we fail quickly but learn from our mistakes?
- Do we accelerate quick wins, and do we pull the plug on ideas that do not make business sense?

Don't be disheartened if the answer to many of the questions above is no. Many firms lack a structured innovation approach. In December 2016 we undertook research among CMOs and heads of business development at leading professional services firms (Beddow, 2017). We asked them about their existing innovation activities and their plans for the future. Our survey reveals that the approach taken by many firms is unstructured and ad hoc, but that the majority have serious aspirations to improve. Key findings include:

- Only 12 per cent have a formal process for testing or co-creating innovation ideas with clients, but 59 per cent would like to implement this in their firm.

- Just 14 per cent have a designated budget for innovation projects in their firm, but 50 per cent would like to introduce one.

- Although 36 per cent currently design joined-up propositions to package their services and expertise to clients in new ways, 56 per cent would like to do this in the near future.

Once you have set your overall innovation strategy and priorities, the next building block is to identify the right team to take them forward. Matthew Whalley, director of legal risk at EY, believes that innovation has to be driven by people with passion: 'Successful innovation always relies on a group of passionate individuals driving something through that they believe in. In my experience you need to have belief and passion to get other people on board and to deal with the bumps and the bruises that come with trying to do things differently.'

Passion is necessary but not sufficient. Effective leaders need to gather a balanced innovation team with a diversity of skills and outlooks. At different points of the innovation lifecycle different mindsets are needed. It is important to have passionate innovators but you also need more objective team members who can identify when the project is going off course. You also need to ensure your innovation team has a balance of skills, notably marketing, technology, process-improvement and supply chain management. There are additional advantages in hiring people from outside professional services, who bring new perspectives and expertise.

## *Phase one – ideation*

Once your innovation strategy has been set and your team put in place, the next task is to create a pipeline of ideas. This is commonly referred to as the 'ideation phase'. Innovations don't arise from lucky accidents. Innovative people and businesses make lots of mistakes and go down many blind alleys. In reality their success comes from having the discipline to take ideas, screen the good from the bad, and commercialize them quickly and profitably. This disciplined approach vastly increases the chances of success.

Where do good ideas come from? From inside your firm or from outside? Fifty years ago a new approach to innovation emerged known as 'open innovation', a term promoted by Henry Chesbrough, the faculty director of the Hass School of Business at the University of California (Chesbrough, 2003). In his view: 'Open innovation is a paradigm that assumes that firms can and should use external ideas as well as internal ideas, and internal and external paths to market, as the firms look to advance their technology.'

Put simply, the boundaries between a firm and its external environment have become more permeable and professionals should embrace the diversity of thought and ideas that a more open approach brings, as represented in Figure 2.3. Good ideas can come from your clients, your collaborators, third parties and your suppliers, not only from your employees. Competitors, other sectors and academia are also important sources of inspiration and dialogue. Open innovators are a special breed: they are open-minded, inquisitive, have excellent networks and are good relationship builders.

**Figure 2.3**  An open innovation network

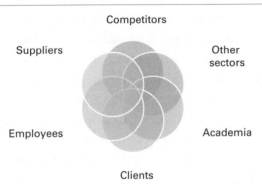

Competitors

Suppliers

Other sectors

Employees

Academia

Clients

For some firms it is important to put a structure around the approach of gathering ideas from staff. Often these innovation hubs take the form of an online platform where employees can pitch an idea or innovation. The brief and guidelines should deliberately remain broad; for example, tell us your ideas about how we can grow the firm. Using online tools employees should be encouraged to review each other's submissions and comment on them. Ideas that pass a certain threshold of comments are then typically examined by more senior members.

Sarah Ducker, Business Development Manager at law firm Irwin Mitchell, has seen first-hand how well innovation hubs can drive engagement and participation: 'In any firm the leadership team have to drive innovation, but everyone should be encouraged to participate, including non-fee-earners. It is useful to give a prize, say vouchers, for winning ideas, but in most cases the fact that an individual's idea has been taken to market is massively motivating in itself. To maximize engagement and discourage cynicism, the way that ideas are captured and evaluated should be transparent and fair.'

Innovators need space for creativity but also constraints. This concept is called the 'sandbox'. A sandbox is not just an area where freestyle play occurs, it is a bounded zone where new ideas can be tested in a fail-quick, fail-safe way. As a leader it is your role to help your colleagues to 'play' as successfully as possible together. This can be done by: setting challenging goals, measures of success and time-tables, allocating finite operational resources and defining the 'concept of operations' (ie the financial resources) and defining responsibilities and activities (see Figure 2.4).

Some firms have taken this sandbox approach one step further by setting up a separate entity at arm's length from the day-to-day operations of the firm to develop and commercialize innovation ideas that could potentially cannibalize elements of the traditional professional service model. One example is global law firm Dentons who have invested in setting up Nextlaw Labs, an innovation venture capital fund whose brief, to quote their website, is 'developing, deploying, and investing in new technologies and processes to transform the practice of law around the world'. Examples of investments made by Nextlaw Labs include Beagle, a contract review process that uses artificial intelligence, QualMet, a legal benchmarking tool for in-house counsel, and Doxly, a legal process management tool.

**Figure 2.4** Sandbox innovation

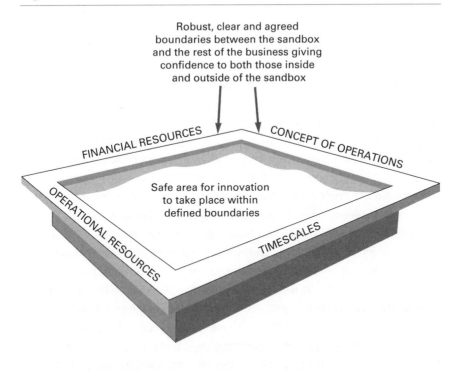

CASE STUDY Creating a space to make innovation happen

As part of our research we interviewed the head of innovation within a global professional services firm. He is specifically tasked with growing the company through innovation by breaking into new markets, creating new products and radically changing models of delivery. When he joined the firm he found a track record of incremental innovation, with partners taking it upon themselves to improve existing processes, usually by trying to find ways to maximize efficiency. This meant, however, that more novel innovations simply weren't being put forward. Many partners were afraid to fail, afraid that they would invest too much time in a project that might not succeed, and see their performance metrics suffer for it.

The challenge, then, was how to create room for innovation, a space where passionate people could pursue projects without having to worry about traditional metrics of success, having their ideas quashed by senior management, or stymied by a lack of collaboration between internal teams.

One of the first initiatives to address the problem was to create an online platform, where any employee of the firm could pitch an idea or innovation. Of all the firm's employees who contributed to the platform, there were several hundred who did so passionately. They were the ones who spent an hour at 11 pm on a Tuesday and three hours on a Sunday morning commenting on multiple ideas. They were the innovators the firm needed to move forward its innovation vision.

Of course it is important to be selective. At least 90 per cent of the firm's employees still had to be focused on the immediate imperative of creating revenue. The critical success factor was to identify innovators without endangering the company's bottom line or engendering resentment from the rest of the workforce.

Once identified, potential innovators had to be given space to flourish. This meant involving management in a supportive way, without crushing ideas with too much top-heavy control. For example, when asked about their strategic focus most of the firm's management would say that it should be on the largest companies. However, what the head of innovation found when he started his platform was that a third of the innovative ideas involved small and medium-sized enterprises. By ignoring those ideas the firm ran the risk of alienating some of its most innovative employees and missing out on key areas of future business.

To square this circle the head of innovation only involved the Board in the most promising innovations. First, all the contributions to the online platform were winnowed down to an A-list, which was then scrutinized by internal panels, which in turn nominated the most promising ideas and presented them to the Board. In order not to discourage the innovators, however, the owners of all A-list ideas were invited to a series of workshops to discuss their ideas, provide feedback and brainstorm ways of improving them.

The head of innovation now runs a team of six people, who scan for ideas, pick one up each, run with it and see if it has potential. This team is encouraged to take risks, and its autonomy means that it can overcome the problem of different internal teams or departments being wary of collaborating with each other. Their experiences shows that innovation is not about finding the best ideas, it is about matching good ideas with people who want to develop them.

## Phase two – prioritize

Once innovation ideas have been generated the next step is to prioritize the good from the bad and the indifferent. Typically ideas should be pitched by an innovation team to a panel of senior managers who will evaluate them and choose which ones to take forward to the next stage of development. Here, professional services firms have a lot to learn from other industries which typically take more disciplined approaches to evaluating innovation potential, including formal decision-gate moments when innovation ideas are evaluated and risk-profiled by the business.

A decision grid (see Figure 1.2 in Chapter 1) is an extremely useful tool to think through all the decisions that will need to be made when launching a new product or service and to formulate a business case for budget approval. At the outset, list all the questions that will need to be answered before launch to determine whether the innovation idea is likely to be successful or not. Each member of the innovation team should share their initial hypotheses on the right way forward. This process clarifies thinking and identifies whether the team are all on the same page or not. It also identifies where more research and analysis may need to be done before an idea will meet the threshold to pass a decision-gate.

Questions you may want to ask yourself to help shape your firm's thinking about a new proposition, include:

- What is the anticipated level of demand for the new offering?
- Where is the 'sweet spot' for the offering? What types of client segments and buyers should we target?
- What steps do we need to take to develop and market the approach internally and externally?
- What is the required delivery model for the proposition?
- How can the idea be successfully scaled up into a viable economic proposition?
- How do we want our clients to feel when buying this offering from us?
- What would differentiate our potential offering from competitors?

## Phase three – prototype

Once the business case has been formulated the next phase is to mock up the service offering as a prototype. People tend to think of proto-types as only applicable to physical products, but the principles can also be applied to new services and this is particularly appropriate for professional services firms where clients tend to buy on track record, relationships and proven successes.

Build a prototype by mocking up how the client would experience the new service offering. This could include developing a website, marketing material and sample outputs. You could even write a script for how staff and clients would interact in key scenarios such as a sales meeting or delivery meeting for the new service.

Prototyping is an important stage that shouldn't be skipped over. It helps your innovation team to visualize exactly what will be needed to deliver the final service before you go to the expense of developing the real thing. Role-playing sales or delivery scenarios is also a good way of anticipating client needs and identifying potential challenges to the new service which can be ironed out before the idea is scaled up.

## Phase four – test

Before any idea is launched you need to force your team to externalize and test their ideas to provide an honest appraisal of its likely success. Just testing innovative ideas with warm contacts is insufficient; they will often give you overly positive feedback.

In our experience client interviews or focus groups represent an efficient way of testing new services prior to launch. Contrary to what some in your firm may think, clients are often honoured to be asked to be involved in such important initiatives, especially if they feel that their ideas will have a direct impact on how the firm will deliver services to them in future.

Any exploratory conversation should be structured. It needs to explore client needs, which firms they use at the moment and to capture their reactions to the prototype, price point and how the service might be marketed. This kind of market insight, especially if supported by a larger online or telephone research exercise, can help you to:

- validate the level of demand and the potential size of the market;
- identify which segments to target;
- design a service that matches what the clients value and need;
- understand the USP and sales messages to use when marketing innovation ideas;
- decide on the best sales channels to get the service to market;
- provide meaningful evidence on which to build a business case;

- reduce bias and assumptions; and

- test alternative service options.

Sarah Ducker of Irwin Mitchell is a fan of this kind of client research: 'We recognize it is sensible to invest some money up front by doing quantitative and qualitative research to make sure our innovation ideas have legs before we spend more money scaling and launching them. We would always go to potential clients to ask to pilot an idea with them.'

Research will provide a dose of realism to your innovation plans. Not only will it enable you to establish likely demand levels, price points and income projects, but will also allow you to get an accurate assessment of the costs of developing the service, as well as the costs of sale and delivery. Even for the very best ideas many professional services firms often underestimate the costs of sale and the length of time it takes to develop a substantial sales pipeline.

## Phase five – scale

Perhaps the greatest milestone for any innovative idea is winning the first client. To encourage a buyer it is often prudent to offer a discounted rate on the understanding that the first engagement is a beta-test: you expect the client to provide detailed feedback to help you continue to refine the approach for future clients.

Having secured an initial client, it is important to prove the concept has a real market by finding at least a handful of people to buy into your service at full price and declare their commitment. Generating client interest and a commitment by several clients to buy a service at a particular cost is the only way to prove that you haven't just got lucky. During this initial phase it is a good idea to try to capture as much feedback as possible from those who don't buy the service, as well as those who do. These market views will deepen understanding of why clients don't buy and what would make potential buyers say yes.

Many innovations die from lack of interest and sustained investment – we call this the 'valley of death' (see Figure 2.5). New ideas are exciting at the beginning. People flock to offer their thoughts, to brainstorm and make plans but quite soon interest lags as the hard work of rollout continues. Many firms suffer from too many initiatives that don't quite take off.

**Figure 2.5**    The innovation 'valley of death'

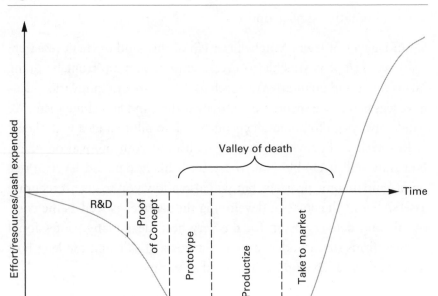

Sustained investment is required to take good ideas and scale them up successfully. However, leaders also need to know when to pull the plug. This requires objective criteria for evaluating which projects should progress and which to terminate, and rigorously enforcing these decisions. In professional services firms it is not uncommon to find that projects that have become the pets of senior people are given time and resources long after they should have been shut down.

## Leaders should cheerlead and challenge innovation

For the six phases of innovation to work in your organization, your role as a leader should be to spend substantial time fostering a culture that accepts the risk of failure, guiding new business ideas and protecting them from managers in the core business who will want to shut them down. Successful leaders encourage an entrepreneurial spirit, not risk for risk's sake. Without supporters among the firm's leadership, it is unlikely that new ideas will attract funding, nor the informal support that is so critical. Leaders should therefore send clear messages to colleagues in their firm that they are expected to refer clients to the new service, offer ideas or lend resources where needed.

Bruce MacMillan, director of the GC Academy at law firm RPC, believes innovative firms need leaders who are prepared to cheerlead as well as to challenge:

> My perception is that many of the most innovative professional firms have had highly inspiring and able managing partners and other leaders who have got elected when they are still 15+ years from their anticipated retirement. This has allowed them personally and corporately to sell and deliver a vision for their firms which is multiyear and, often, over multiple electoral terms rather than solely focused in one-year returns and drawings. They encourage others to develop and bid for resources to test out innovative ideas but have a low tolerance for letting unproven ideas progress without a solid business case.

---

**SUMMARY** Top tips for embracing innovation within your firm

### Set internal expectations about what types of innovation are right for your firm

Think strategically about innovation and communicate your intent to colleagues. It is important that people throughout your firm know where they should focus their time and effort: on incremental innovation to improve efficiency or on radical innovations that will fundamentally change how they work with clients, or a mix of the two. The right approach for your firm will partly depend on your partners and their risk appetite, and on the particular competitive pressures in your market. If your market is becoming increasingly commoditized, radical innovation may be necessary.

### Embrace good ideas, wherever they might originate

Successful innovators reach out to staff, clients and suppliers for new ideas and always have one eye on competitors for alternative solutions that may spur a new innovation. Innovation ideas can be captured formally – through structured conversations, or online platforms – or through informal channels. However, it is important to have a structured process in play to evaluate ideas when they are brought to you.

### Give employees licence to engage in 'structured innovation play'

Employees who recognize the value of spending time on innovation are more likely to find opportunities in their busy schedules to set aside dedicated innovation time. However, even the brightest and best need to be given some parameters to focus their efforts. As a leader you need to set some ground rules. What is the innovation goal you want people to focus on? What activities and resources do you expect them to make use of to achieve that goal? Without some innovation structure, employees are less likely to generate successful ideas.

### Encourage prototyping and rigorous innovation decision-making

Before going to the expense of creating a new service or developing a new business model, it is a worthwhile investment of time and effort to create a prototype. Rather than aim for a 100 per cent prototype, encourage a 'good enough' mentality whereby people get feedback from potential buyers early in the process to iron out glitches as they progress. Successful innovators keep pushing their ideas forward and don't get distracted. However, the best innovators also know when to say no to pet projects that have no proven business case.

### Involve clients at all phases of the innovation lifecycle

It can be tempting to build and refine innovation ideas behind closed doors, launching them in the market when a firm believes it has designed a perfect solution. Too few professional services firms involve clients in the design, testing to gather valuable insight to determine the potential size of your market, propensity to buy and priority target-market segments for business development.

# References

Allen & Overy (2014) *Unbundling a Market: The appetite for new legal services models*. Available from: www.allenovery.com/publications [accessed 16 March 2017]

Altman Weil (2016) *Law Firms in Transition: A flash survey*. Available from: www.altmanweil.com [accessed 16 March 2017]

Beddow, Alastair (2017) Turning client focus into competitive advantage, *PM Magazine*, January. Available from www.pmforum.co.uk/knowedge/surveys/marketing-benchmark/marketing-benchmark-2017.aspx [accessed 16 March 2017]

Best, Jo (2013) IBM Watson: the inside story of how the Jeopardy-winning supercomputer was born, and what it wants to do next, TechRepublic. Available from: www.techrepublic.com/article/ibm-watson-the-inside-story-of-how-the-jeopardy-winning-supercomputer-was-born-and-what-it-wants-to-do-next/ [accessed 16 March 2017]

Chesbrough, Henry William (2003) *Open Innovation: The new imperative for creating and profiting from technology*, Harvard Business School Press, Boston

# Performance:  03
# how to improve
# the profitability of
# client engagements

As we have shown in the previous two chapters, within Business Leadership successful leaders create a compelling vision for their firm that clearly articulates strategic choices and innovation opportunities to unlock future growth. However, successful leaders also know that sound day-to-day financial management is essential for generating the profits that will be needed to fund these growth strategies and innovations.

This chapter describes the levers at the disposal of professional services leaders to improve financial performance in their firm. Using a fictionalized example of a private client department in a typical professional services firm, we illustrate the impact of pulling different profit levers and the trade-offs involved to secure a balance that works for employers and clients as well as the bottom line.

## The eight profit levers for professional services firms

Professionals tend to focus on a small number of financial metrics to assess how well the firm is performing. These metrics have an incredibly powerful influence over the way leaders think and behave, and the expectations they set for others in the firm. Utilization is one example; put simply, utilization is the proportion of somebody's time spent on work that is billable to a client. If somebody is 100 per cent utilized they would expect to charge every single hour they work to a client.

Utilization is clearly important. If somebody is not sufficiently utilized over a sustained period of time they may not generate sufficient client billings to pay their salary costs, let alone make profit for the firm. However, focusing on metrics such as utilization in isolation can be dangerous because it doesn't allow you to see the bigger picture of where and how your firm makes money. A narrow focus on metrics can inadvertently create a barrier to senior partners delegating work to the appropriate level of fee-earner, or cross-selling work to colleagues. Even worse, professionals can be discouraged from investing sufficient time in business development or skills development because they are anxious to hit their chargeable hours targets.

In our experience firms that take a more nuanced approach understand that there is a range of levers that can be pulled to increase financial performance. They know that a long-term sustainable solution to increasing profitability is rarely just to work people for longer hours. Figure 3.1 illustrates eight profit levers within three broad categories: structure, time management and client management.

The 'structure' levers relate to the operational model by which your firm delivers client work. Some firms and some types of work necessitate a highly leveraged model, in which a single partner manages a large team of juniors; in other firms and for other types of work it is appropriate to have a single partner and just one or two juniors working together. Both of these models can be profitable, but only if the model is correctly aligned with the nature of the work and the kind of value the client is willing to pay for.

**Figure 3.1**    The eight profit levers for professional firms

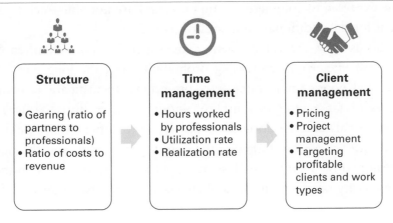

Increasingly, professional services firms have looked at their revenue-to-cost ratio to find ways of delivering the same calibre of work with a cheaper operating model. The most common solution for firms has been to move staff members out of expensive cities like London, where salary and real estate costs are high, to lower-cost cities such as Manchester, Belfast and Glasgow where quality talent is available to deliver work in a more cost-effective way. However, making large-scale changes to the operating model to reduce costs over the long-term is likely to require some initial investment so profitability benefits may not be accrued in the first year of the change.

'Time management' levers relate to how professionals spend their time and what proportion of that is chargeable to clients. One of the simplest levers to pull is to work people harder by expecting them to put more hours on the clock and spend more of their time on chargeable work. This may be workable in the short-term but over a longer period risks burning out staff and reducing time available for other essential activities such as business development.

The fifth lever, 'realization rate', relates to the amount of potentially chargeable time that is actually recovered from clients. For example, although an accountant may work 100 hours completing an audit for a client, she may only get paid for 70 of these. The realization rate is 70 per cent. Client engagements may have low realization rates for lots of reasons. In some instances this may be because junior people are being brought up to speed with a particular technical skill and it is not considered appropriate to bill a client for this 'learning' time. However, in many instances, low realization occurs because of poor scoping and project management: professionals underestimate the time expected to complete certain tasks and are not able to charge a client for the additional hours out of scope.

This is why the three 'client management' levers can often be the most effective at increasing profitability over the long term. As discussed, poor scoping, pricing and project management are the major causes of large write-offs in professional services firms. However, professionals may be doomed at the outset to suffer low profitability if they are poor at targeting the right types of client and the right types of work. That is why leaders need to set a strategic vision that gives clarity on the right types of clients and work to target in order

**Figure 3.2** The eight profit lever model

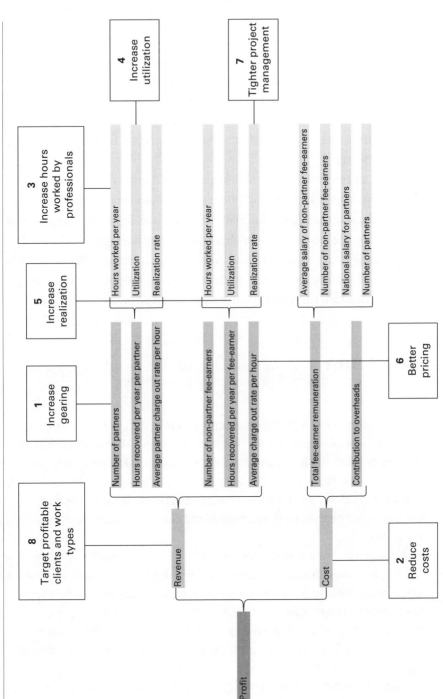

to generate the desired level of profitable growth for the firm, and to be decisive in saying no to targeting low profitability and low growth potential market segments.

To illustrate how manipulating these eight levers affects profitability we have developed a financial model that illustrates in a simple way how small changes to any of the eight factors can change profits (see Figure 3.2). This model can be used to inform strategic planning or as a diagnostic tool to assess where to focus performance improvements.

In its simplest form, profit is calculated by taking revenue and deducting costs, including fee-earner remuneration and contribution to the overheads of the firm. The revenue figure is derived from calculating the number of professionals and partners multiplied by the average charge out rate and the number of hours recovered. The number of hours recovered is derived from the hours worked per year adjusted by the utilization and realization rates.

**CASE STUDY** Improve performance of a private client practice with below average profitability

The eight lever model is perhaps best understood by using a fictionalized example of a private client practice at a law firm. Following a change of leadership, the new department's lead partner, Amanda, has pledged to increase profitability under her leadership. Although the team is well-respected by colleagues in other parts of the firm, revenues have been flat in the last three years as the market has become more competitive and clients are increasingly cost conscious.

Amanda's practice area has four partners, including herself, and seven other fee-earners. Revenues for the last year were £2.4 million. However, after taking into account the practice area's contribution to overheads the private client team made just under £300,000 in profits. This is a net margin of 12 per cent below the profit margins achieved by comparable firms and other departments in this firm. The financial position before Amanda took charge is illustrated in Figure 3.3 opposite.

Amanda has the eight levers of profitability at her disposal. Which will result in increased profits and which may cause unintended consequences?

**Figure 3.3** Amanda's private client practice before making changes

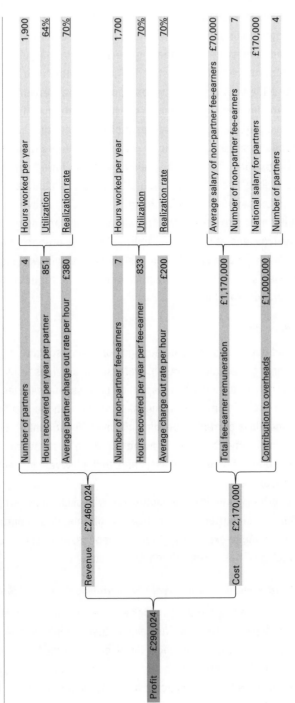

### Lever 1: increase gearing

Poor profitability is often caused by having too many partners and directors and not enough junior staff. Once you take into account their lower salaries, junior and mid-level staff can actually generate better margins per-hour-worked than partners and senior staff. In Amanda's team the gearing ratio is just under 2:1, which is pretty low for a professional services firm. Better delegation, and increasing the numbers of junior staff, may therefore significantly improve profit margins. However, increasing gearing has its difficulties. Amanda needs to make sure quality is maintained if more junior staff are recruited. Proper use of checklists, training and mentoring can help. However, achieving a higher level of gearing will often require a change in the role of the equity partner. Amanda and her fellow partners may have to shift their mindset away from maximizing their personal billings and doing most of the work themselves, and at 64 per cent utilized they are probably not delegating enough work. Instead, they will need to spend more time winning new work and supervising others. Training and coaching may be required to help bring about this behavioural shift.

### Lever 2: reduce costs

Many firms let overheads creep up during boom years so there is often scope for some trimming. As a rule of thumb, professional services firms should aim for 40–50 per cent of turnover being spent on professional salaries, 30 per cent on overheads (including non-professional salaries), with the rest as profit (20–30 per cent). Amanda is currently spending just over 40 per cent of revenue on overheads, which suggests there is scope to reduce costs overall; for example, by cutting the number of personal assistants to the lawyers by centralizing secretarial resources.

Cutting overheads needs to be undertaken with skill. Short-term cost cutting can undermine the long-term competitiveness of Amanda's department. Her clients will continue to expect a high-quality service, more skilled advisers and better technology. These areas all require investment.

### Levers 3, 4 and 5: increase hours worked by professionals and their utilization

One option available to Amanda is to look at how the professionals in her department use their time. Top City law firms expect their lawyers to charge at least 1,600 hours per year, with some Magic Circle and US firms having even higher targets, closer to 2,000 hours. In Amanda's case the hours worked by professionals in her team are within the expected ballpark, but utilization and realization rates are fairly low. This means that although non-partners are working 1,700 hours on average per year, only 833 (or 49 per cent) hours are chargeable.

One relatively pain-free way of improving utilization and chargeable hours is to make sure all the time spent working on a client matter is fully recorded. This can be a particular problem when professionals work on many small matters and have to switch from one matter to another, as might be the case for Amanda's team if they work on lots of small jobs for many different private clients.

A good time-recording system can help. The latest software can watch what fee-earners do and prompts them to record time correctly. There should be a clear and understandable time-recording policy detailing what should be recorded and in what category. This should include frequently asked questions and how to deal with grey areas. It may be that training is needed to support the policy or the introduction of a new time-recording system.

For Amanda, getting her colleagues to record time properly could have a major improvement on profitability. Adding 5 per cent to the utilization of both partners and professionals in Figure 3.3 increases profits from £290,024 to £474,404, a jump of more than 60 per cent.

### Lever 6: better pricing

Alternative fee structures have become commonplace within professional services firms as clients have become less tolerant of hourly rates. One solution for Amanda is simply to increase charge out rates but unless her team is widely considered by clients to be less expensive than other equivalent private client firms, this is not likely to be welcomed. A more appropriate solution may be to investigate alternative pricing arrangements and to consider shifting a greater proportion of work that her team undertakes from an hourly rate to alternative fee arrangements.

The key to making this shift work profitably is to understand that each type of fee arrangement requires a change in the way professionals work, and a team capable of effectively managing the risk of over-runs. Amanda, therefore, needs to understand each element of the cost of delivering a legal matter for clients. The more detailed this understanding is the better. Each of these cost elements should be linked to a time-recording system to provide real-time information about hours spent on tasks against budget.

Broadly speaking, there are four distinct pricing models used by professional services firms: hourly rate, fixed fee, success-based and blended. We have seen professional services firms with pricing guides that list more than 50 fee structures, yet each was simply a variation on the four structures overleaf. Table 3.1 summarizes where each of these fee arrangements might be most appropriate, and the critical success factors for managing engagements profitably using each fee structure.

**Table 3.1** Four fee structures for professional firms

| | Hourly rate | Fixed fee | Success-based | Blended |
|---|---|---|---|---|
| **What does it reward?** | Input – ie the more hours spent, the higher the fee. | Output – ie delivering to an agreed scope of work for an agreed fee. | Outcome – ie achieving a strategic business or personal goal for a client. | A blend of inputs, outputs and/or outcomes. |
| **Example of pricing structures** | Time and materials. Cost plus margin. | Fixed price. Capped fees. | Conditional fee agreements. Success bonus. | Blend of pricing mechanisms. |
| **Who owns risk?** | Client – an inefficient engagement means a higher bill. | Firm – an inefficient engagement means lower profitability. | Shared – an inefficient engagement means outcome might not be achieved. | Shared – a blended approach. |
| **When is this fee structure most appropriate?** | Where there is uncertainty of outcome and the client has control of the process. Example: dispute resolution. | Where there is an element of certainty over the outputs and the resources required to achieve that output. Examples: audit, conveyancing. | Where there is a tangible measure of success dependent on the quality of advice delivered. Examples: debt recovery, tax planning. | Where there are different elements of the scope that can be matched to different fee structures. |
| **What are the critical success factors for making this fee structure profitable?** | 1. High staff utilization. 2. Thorough time recording. 3. High recovery rate. | 1. Tight project planning and scoping. 2. Process automation and technology. 3. Proper delegation of tasks to lower cost fee-earners. | 1. Clarity of outcome at outset of engagement. 2. Sufficient risks management and controls. 3. Regular communication with client. | Depends on the blend of pricing structures used. |
| **How to focus scope of work** | Clarity of desired outcomes, governance and communications. | Clarity of outputs, team roles and scope boundaries (ie what is out of scope). | Clarity of the roles, responsibilities of the client and the firm. | Depends on the blend of pricing structures used. |

There are several options open to Amanda to improve pricing beyond changing the fee structure being used. First there may be an opportunity for her team to articulate more clearly how their advice creates value for clients. For example, the team's inheritance-planning advice should save clients money or time in the long term: if Amanda and her team can make clients understand the value delivered, clients might be less likely to quibble about the headline price.

As a department leader, Amanda could give her colleagues better guidance and develop stronger governance and protocols to ensure pricing is sustainable and consistent across the team. It is not uncommon for professionals to have their own idiosyncratic ways of pricing up jobs even within teams doing the same kinds of work for similar clients. Using appropriate pricing mechanisms more consistently is a proven way to deliver higher margins.

### Lever 7: tighten up project management

Low realization rates are caused by a large difference in the number of hours worked and the number of hours that can be billed to a client. This is most often caused by heavy discounting at the outset of an engagement, writing off large numbers of hours at the end along with poor project management and scoping. If Amanda was able to increase her average realization for partners and other staff from 70 per cent to 85 per cent, then profit would increase from £290,024 to £817,172.

To do this, Amanda will need to tighten up on scoping and project management in her team. The starting point might be educating her colleagues on the damage this is currently doing to profitability: in our experience professionals discount fees or undertake out-of-scope work without understanding how much it damages profitability. Figure 3.4 shows the various ways that profits can leak away throughout a client engagement. What looks on paper at the outset to be a profitable piece of work can quickly become less profitable due to poor scope and project management.

Getting basic project and process management disciplines right can really help to plug profit leakage. Amanda can work with the professionals in her team to develop a series of straightforward tools adapted to their particular practice area. In our experience four tools are particularly useful: a pricing model, a process map, a plan on a page, and a fees schedule.

Interactive pricing models can be generated relatively simply on Excel. The aim is to help professionals price their work profitably by identifying the main phases of a client matter, the individual tasks required within each page, who will undertake the task, and time estimates for each individual team member.

**Figure 3.4**  Profit leakage across the client lifecycle

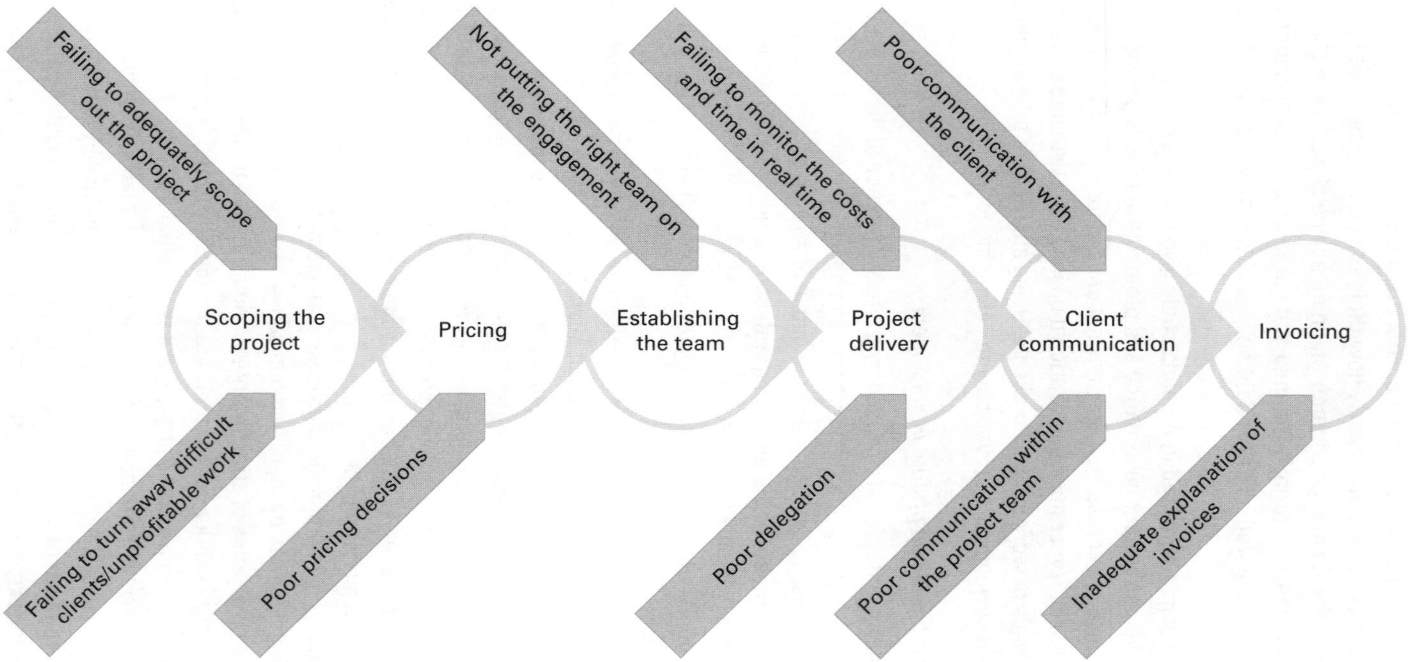

Staff often underestimate the time it takes to complete tasks. This is known as the 'planning fallacy': we typically expect tasks to take less time than they actually do because we base our estimates on one standout memory – our best past experience – rather than the average time it has taken to do similar tasks in the past. A pricing model can overcome this problem by building in realistic estimates and time assumptions based on analysis of past performance for similar work.

If Amanda's team find clients regularly pushing back on price, the tool can be used to discuss ways of re-scoping the work rather than cutting the margin. Work can be re-scoped by getting the client to undertake tasks, missing out some tasks altogether or getting the work done at a more junior level. Clients are generally happy to have these open conversations about price and scope at the outset of a project.

Process mapping is a valuable exercise for teams that carry out similar types of work on a regular basis. A process map highlights the different steps involved in carrying out the work, including correspondence, meetings and iterations of documents; this helps to understand where time is wasted and where opportunities to standardize processes or introduce templates could make tangible improvements to profitability.

John Rowley, a former tax director at KPMG and now a specialist in project management for professional services firms, has seen this approach deliver real value in many firms:

> In my experience professional firms are usually poor at self-evaluation and at identifying opportunities for process improvement: they believe that each client and each piece of work is unique so that process improvements cannot be made. In reality, this is not true – even high value consultancy engagements often involve up to 70 per cent repeatable processes. Simply by redesigning a couple of processes, taking out redundant steps or looking at tactical resourcing issues firms can make a huge difference to their overall profitability.
>
> Multiple iterations of tasks and documents is an endemic issue in professional firms, and one that invariably reduces profitability. In one firm an element of a tax return process was unnecessarily repeated over 20 times before it was completed, each time involving communications between the client and adviser and adding to cost. Mapping out this process based on a review of recently completed client files was highly illuminating for the tax leadership: they hadn't appreciated how much time was wasted, and how much of the work done differed from internal guidelines.

When professionals are successful in a client pitch the temptation is for everybody to get their heads down and start work without properly finalizing the scope or work or communicating a proper project plan to the client. A simple

**Figure 3.5** Amanda's private client practice after making changes

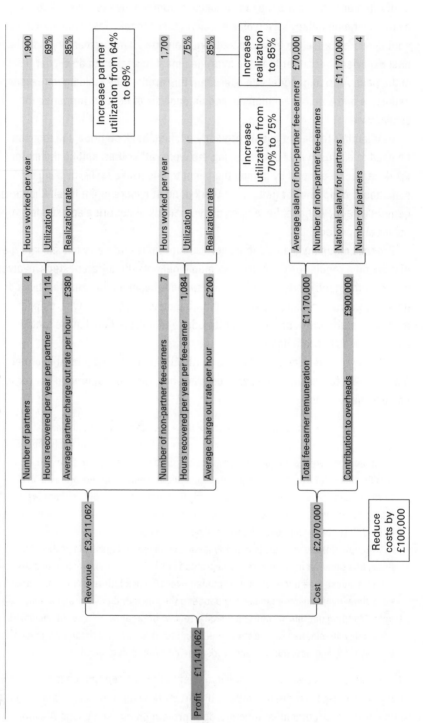

template plan, possibly on a single page, can be a valuable discussion tool at the outset of a client engagement to frame a conversation about the different stages of a matter, timetable, scope, risks and critical success factors. Keeping key information to a page or two makes this a useful reference document for client and adviser as the work progresses.

Clearly setting out what tasks are in scope and what will be treated as out-of-scope extras makes it easier to have a conversation about changing the budget if the scope changes in the middle of an assignment. Use this scoping conversation as an opportunity to make it clear what the client needs to deliver to achieve deadlines and by when, and what the mechanism will be for determining whether additional requests are out of scope. This 'no surprises' approach requires some up-front investment in time but it can pay dividends later on in terms of greater efficiency, reduced scope creep and more prompt payment of fees.

Leaders should encourage their finance teams to provide professionals with real-time data on fees and for professionals to communicate this information regularly to clients. A simple breakdown showing how fees accrued compare with an original estimate, and the tasks that have been completed, will often be sufficient for clients. The task of updating clients could be delegated to a relatively junior member of staff but it needs to be done consistently.

### Lever 8: target profitable clients and work types

Once Amanda has looked at her cost base and the efficiency of her team, the next place to look is the client base for her department. She could undertake some analysis to explore which clients are profitable and which ones lose money. If there are particular client segments that are consistently unprofitable, there may need to be some hard decisions taken about exiting those types of work or client and using the time saved to focus on business development efforts on more profitable client segments. These analytics can then be used to help develop a better pricing mechanism for future engagements.

### Result: delivering a fourfold profit boost for the private client department

By pulling a combination of these profit levers Amanda can deliver a fourfold increase in profits to her team. The combined impact of trimming overheads by £100,000 and improving utilization and realization rates is to increase profit from £290,024 to £1,141,062 (see Figure 3.5). This healthy net margin of 36 per cent has been achieved without putting up prices or making any professionals redundant.

# Enhancing profitability through cultural change

Improving financial performance is not just about making the right operational and financial choices, it is also about leadership and culture change. Clare Singleton has held senior operations roles at firms including Deloitte and Taylor Wessing. She has observed that the best leaders set high expectations:

> In my experience the firms that set clear and ambitious financial targets are more likely to hit them because it gives people a sense of purpose and a common goal to aim towards. A good place for any firm to focus its profit improvement plan is to ask whether the firm's finance goals are reflected in individual partners' and fee-earners' goals and remuneration. For example, performance management systems sometimes reward professionals for hitting utilization or revenue targets but do not directly reward the team for hitting profit targets.

Although most people in professional services firms accept the theoretical case for better delegation, pricing and project management, they are uncomfortable using the new techniques and don't have the confidence to have frank conversations with clients about scoping and pricing. Professionals can be squeamish about focusing on profitability. However, without a competitive level of profitability it becomes harder to pay the salaries to attract the right talent, and without the right talent it is hard to win quality work and clients.

Getting your team comfortable with having open conversations about pricing and scoping with their clients involves a change in mindset. Some of the commonly cited barriers are outlined in Figure 3.6. To overcome these barriers will probably require a mix of education, confidence-building and practical tools. Providing simple guidance on the economics of professional services firms, including the impact of different pricing mechanisms, charge out rates, leverage and write-offs on profit margin can revolutionize how professionals think about financial performance. Training and support designed around real client scenarios can help professionals to build the confidence to have open conversations with clients, so they feel able to negotiate a fair price without jeopardizing their client relationships.

**Figure 3.6** Common mindset barriers to profitability improvement

'I don't understand financial fundamentals'

'Project management is too onerous'

'I don't feel confident enough to have difficult conversations with clients'

'I'm not incentivized to manage projects profitably'

'I don't have the right information or tools'

'I find it difficult to say no to a client'

'It's impossible to scope my work'

This chapter has focused on profitability, but there are good profits and bad profits. If the strategies outlined above are implemented in a heavy-handed or overly restrictive way they can damage the long-term success of a firm's practice. Pushing up utilization can burn out staff and make clients feel that their bills are being padded out with low-value activity. Heavy-handed cost-cutting destroys morale and reduces long-term productivity as investment in systems and infrastructure suffers.

The skill of a leader is in knowing how to balance the needs of the business to make money against the interests of your firm's people and clients. As George Bull, senior tax partner at accountancy firm RSM acknowledges, sustainable profits result from a long-term outlook and an understanding that the financial management of your firm needs to fit its culture and strategy: 'We are all driven by the financial outcomes, but they are lagging indicators. A lead indicator would be how does a fee-earner feel when she's just come out of a partner's room to be told that there's this new piece of work and she's got to do it?'

**SUMMARY** Top tips for improving profitability and financial performance

### Align your economic model with your culture and types of work

If you compete for high-margin, cutting-edge work, expect high charge-out rates, low leverage and significant investment in learning and development. By contrast, if you compete in price-sensitive market segments, focus attention on improving leverage and utilization but recognize that you will need to invest in systems and technology to achieve efficiency. There is no one-size-fits-all solution. Most professional services firms will operate a series of different economic models for different clients and types of work.

### Don't fixate on utilization and chargeable hours

Although these measures are very important, if they are the only financial metrics you look at you may gain a one-dimensional view of what drives profitability in your firm. Look at the eight levers of profitability to understand alternative strategies for improving financial performance that strike the right balance between profitability, client service and employee morale.

### Make everybody accountable for their financial impact

Profit management should not just be the job of senior partners. All front line staff should understand how the firm makes money, how their actions influence profitability and what they need to do to improve financial performance. Making financial information as transparent as possible and available in real time will enable people to make adjustments to how they service clients to prevent excessive profit leakage on assignments.

### Encourage effective scoping and budgeting conversations

Ensure your staff have at their disposal a good quality pricing tool and are confident in scoping work and dealing with scope creep. Analyse how work is undertaken to identify where to eliminate waste and improve consistency and quality; many professional services firms often have too many senior professionals and don't delegate enough work. Ultimately, profitability will only be improved if your staff are comfortable negotiating fees and ensuring clients are happy to pay a reasonable fee for extra work delivered.

**Don't tolerate low profitability without a reasoned business case**

Sometimes there are valid reasons for continuing to support lower profitability clients or types of work. They may bring prestige or reputation for your firm so their value transcends the amount you are able to bill them. Alternatively, some clients may be good referrers of work, from whom you can move into adjacent markets to secure future revenue streams. However, if there are no justifiable reasons you should not continue to support low profitability work or client types without a realistic plan in place to improve future profitability in these areas.

# PART TWO
# **Client Leadership**

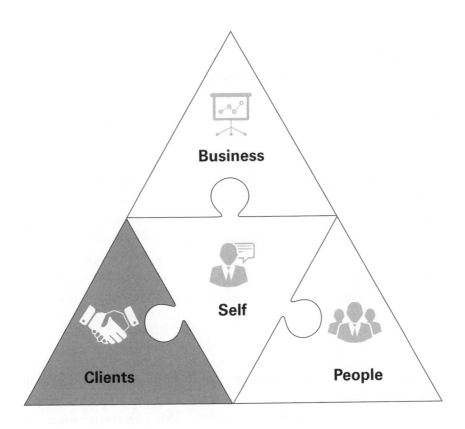

*The more adaptable your firm, the better placed you are to respond to changes among your clients and markets. The best leaders consciously review their strategy so they are better placed to deal with change. I can think of a number of firms who haven't met that level of adaptability and therefore have become ossified. Often this inflexibility is caused by a lack of leadership vision. It seems to me that a firm's leadership has a fantastically important role to play to communicate a vision about where the firm is going and the kinds of clients the firm wants to work with. That vision lifts people, it gives them a sense of certainty and security, dynamism and direction. It shows them that the firm isn't drifting, but that there is clarity about where they should focus their business development and client relationship efforts.*

JAMES PARTRIDGE, SENIOR PARTNER AT THOMSON, SNELL & PASSMORE

*To be a good leader you definitely need to know your firm's clients very well, and really listen to them. You need to look out for their needs and where you can join people together internally to serve clients better. You need to know what your clients want from your firm because that influences a lot of the decisions you take as a leader such as the direction you decide to take the firm, and where you invest time and money. If you don't listen to your clients then you won't drive your business forward in a way that meets the needs of your clients.*

JOANNA WORBY, MANAGING PARTNER AT BRACHERS

The opportunity to deliver high-quality, intellectually stimulating work for a varied range of clients is often what attracts many people to embark on a career in the professions. Although the transition to leader will likely mean that the proportion of your time spent on fee-earning work reduces as you shift your focus towards other leadership priorities, clients remain a critical component of any leader's role in a professional services firm. Without an in-depth understanding of the clients and markets you wish your firm to work with, how their needs are changing and what they expect from their relationships with the professionals in your firm, it is very difficult to set a strategy that will generate a sustainable workflow and income over the long term.

In the last couple of decades the client–adviser relationship has moved from being cosy, gentlemanly and benign to far more formalized, rigorous and value-oriented. Although the person-to-person element of the relationship remains integral to success, a much more diverse range of factors influence buying behaviour than ever before. As technical expertise has been reduced to a hygiene factor, not a differentiator, clients place greater emphasis on the quality of the experience of working with professionals. They focus on ease of doing business, value for money and whether the service delivered is coordinated and efficient.

Following the global financial crisis clients began to think much harder about how they spent their money, where they could extract value from professional advisers and what tasks they were able to do in-house. As more professionals have opted for a career in-house, the knowledge and skills within in-house functions such as finance and legal have risen exponentially, which in turn has caused client organizations to become more savvy about what they are buying and how much they are willing to pay. With a new ecosystem of professional services delivery models now well-established, clients are free to pick and choose exactly what type of firm they want to deliver which part of a job, and at what price. Into this mix has stepped the power of procurement: decision-makers who are less influenced by the personal touch and who prioritize dispassionate criteria such as relevant experience, price and team make-up. Even strategic or advisory services are being challenged on price as never before.

As a result of these changes the mystique once enjoyed by professional firms has been demystified and the balance of power in the relationship has shifted towards clients. They want to be more involved in scoping work, setting the terms of engagements, and measuring the performance of their professional firms. Although clients still value long-term, trusted relationships – often preferring to work with a small group of firms they value as genuine business partners, not just technical advisers – they will not tolerate below-par performance. Successful leaders of professional firms know there are competitors hungry to eat their lunch, and so take steps to ensure their firm's client relationships are 'sticky' and not dependent on the efforts of a single individual in the firm.

Added to this already challenging environment is the impact of technology and automation, which has fuelled the fire of the 'more for less' mantra. As many professional firms promise that technology can speed up the delivery of services and reduce the need for large delivery teams, clients expect cost-savings to be passed on to them and for their professional advisers to spend more of their time focused on valued-added activities. So where do these changes leave the traditional relationship model? It has become clear that the changes precipitated by the 2008 financial crisis are not a cyclical blip. As a former partner at a top-20 law firm recently told us, 'Everybody feels that clients have tasted blood and are not prepared to go back to the old days. Procurement is now a profession: they walk in and you face a battle. It feels like you are taking a knife into a gun fight!'

Firms that find new ways to engage with their clients and differentiate how they deliver their services, will be able to successfully position themselves as one of the 'go-to' firms in their respective market. As a leader it is your role to define how you want the people in your firm to work with their clients. You have a responsibility to champion the voice of the client internally and to consider the client perspective when taking strategic and operational decisions that will affect how people work and behave. Without strong client leadership, professional firms risk becoming too internally focused and too slow to respond to how clients want to shape their future working relationship.

## Key questions considered in Client Leadership

In the three chapters in the Client Leadership section we will explore answers and best practices for the following questions:

In *Understanding: how to stay attuned to the changing needs of your clients and markets* we answer:

- How do you understand which client segments contribute most to your firm financially and in other ways?

- How do you develop deep insights about the clients you work for today and the ones you want to work for tomorrow?

- How can you best capture feedback from clients about their experience of working with your firm?

In *Connecting: how to foster a client-focused culture in your firm* we consider:

- How do you champion a client-focused culture within your firm?
- How do you encourage collaborative relationships with clients and draw on the views of clients to co-create solutions?
- How do you develop from transactional relationships with clients to high-value, long-term trusted relationships?

In *Sales: how to improve your firm's client-development success* we answer:

- How do you lead and manage your sales pipeline to win the right work for your firm?
- How do you identify the best opportunities to pursue?
- How do you positively influence decision-makers within client organizations?

# Understanding: 04
# how to stay
# attuned to the
# changing needs
# of your clients
# and markets

Professional services firms are full of intelligent, perceptive individuals who are trained to understand and resolve complex problems for their clients. However, they do not always apply the same rigour to understanding their clients as they do to their technical competencies. The nature of the professional mindset and the technical training that professionals receive, means that they are typically most comfortable operating in the domain of precedent. Professionals prefer not to challenge the status quo unless there are very compelling reasons to do so; they find a client type they enjoy working with and can make money from, or structure their projects in a particular way, and rarely stray from this familiar formula.

Ironically, being too comfortable in a given niche can sometimes be a barrier to developing a deeper understanding of clients. Professionals can rely on assumptions rather than asking questions to understand the specific needs of a particular client. Research that we have conducted into the relationship between clients and their professional firms has shown that a lack of understanding of a client's business is the top factor likely to damage the professional relationship; this is cited by a higher proportion of clients as potentially damaging to the relationship (52 per cent cite this as one of the top three most damaging factors) than the provision of inappropriate advice or slow response to communication (both cited by 45 per cent) (Financial Times, Meridian West and MPF 2012).

As we have made clear throughout, both the professional services ecosystem and the way that clients interact with their professional advisers have undergone, and will continue to undergo, rapid change. Professional firms cannot afford to stand still and rely on business as usual to set them on a path to future prosperity. Leaders of professional firms need to initiate conversations with their colleagues about how their firm works with its clients, and to encourage others to develop a nuanced understanding of their clients' changing needs. This chapter is designed to help leaders promote a better understanding of their firm's chosen clients, including how to identify the strongest opportunities for making money and deepening relationships further, and how to use feedback from clients to inform strategic leadership decisions.

## Client profitability: understand high priority client segments

The first step in the Bow Tie process for developing a strategy, outlined in Chapter 1, is to analyse your current clients and markets and to anticipate how these may change in future. In Chapter 1 we focused on how to make informed decisions about the client segments that represent the strongest future growth potential for your firm, and the sources of information you can use to build a strong evidence base for that decision. Here we focus on how analysing your existing client base will help your firm to understand where it makes money and which client segments should be considered high priority. Taking an objective view of your client relationships in this way – instead of relying on personal and subjective hunches – will help you to understand which client segments generate most profit, and where you should make your biggest investments to grow future business.

Professional services firms typically look at internally focused financial metrics. They measure revenue and profit generated by individual fee-earners, teams or practice areas, but in our experience relatively few firms analyse revenue and profit generated by individual clients or client segments. Those who do tend to do this based on available data for a small number of key accounts, or based on simple segmentation such as industry sector, company type or client location. With this information they are able to tell which types of client drive steady income for the firm and which are more cyclical. This information also makes it easier to spot trends in the way that certain client segments typically work with the firm, and which practice areas or technical disciplines sell most to which types of client.

Analysing data by client segment helps professional firms to identify where they might be chasing profitless prosperity. Larger client revenues are not always a sign of profitable relationships. Multiple projects and the cost of winning and managing a diverse portfolio of projects for a single client can quickly undermine profitability, especially if this time-allocation is not accounted for in the way firms price their work. It is not uncommon for firms to over-service their largest clients but at the same time to cut prices by offering volume discounts to maintain the flow of work. Financial services sector clients, for example, may generate significant amounts of revenue for a firm, but require a big investment in relationship development and project management time, which cannot always be fully recovered from the client. On the surface financial services may look like a highly lucrative client sector to pursue, but a more detailed analysis might suggest profit potential is lower than expected.

One way of representing this information is the client portfolio-assessment tool (see Figure 4.1) which compares the revenue and profitability of different client segments. This visual representation will enable you to easily see which client segments fall into your 'sweet spot', high revenue/high profit clients. These clients require investment to keep them warm and loyal to ensure they continue to use your firm when they need external advice in future.

Clients or client segments that fall into the low revenue/low profit quadrant need to be interrogated further to understand whether there is a realistic potential for future revenue growth or whether there are more efficient ways to work with them to boost profitability. If not, is there a strategic reason for continuing to service this client or client segment?

**Figure 4.1**   Client portfolio-assessment tool

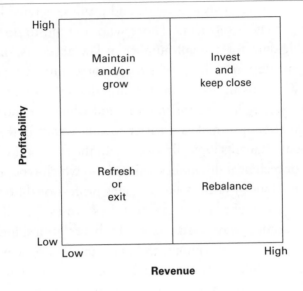

For example, they might be brand enhancing or a key referrer of other types of client and therefore justify the investment of time to maintain the relationship; more factors to consider are outlined in Figure 4.2. However, if there is no compelling strategic case to make, you should seriously consider exiting that particular client or client segment as it is losing the firm money and not delivering any strategic value.

**Figure 4.2**   Client relationship factors

## Client relationship factors

### Profitable

Which client segments generate recurring profits over time? Which clients are likely to introduce you to other profitable clients or use multiple service lines?

### Long-term

Which clients have the potential to grow into long-term, sustainable relationships? Which clients see you as a sounding-board to develop ideas for future projects, and which will appoint you via a structured procurement process on a project by project basis?

### Challenge

Which clients will stretch your firm's capabilities and will provide interesting and challenging work to help your team members to develop their skills?

### Fresh

Which clients will help you refresh your firm's thinking and innovate your service offering to stay ahead of competitors? Which clients are dynamic and growing, and will try to disrupt the status quo and are therefore open to testing any new innovations you develop?

### Culture

Which clients are a good fit for your firm's style, culture and way of working? Which clients are brand-enhancing for your firm?

Some firms at the vanguard of client understanding have made significant changes to how they capture and report management information about their clients. This includes new ways to segment clients and a greater emphasis on thinking about clients as individual buyers and influencers, not just as organizations. Segmentation categories used by forward-thinking firms include buyer type (comparing functional buyers such as in-house lawyers, strategic buyers such as CEOs, and influencers such as non-executive directors (NEDs)), length of relationship, number of services used, and number of relationship touchpoints with the firm. For example, is there a correlation between the length of an individual's relationship with your firm and the number of services they typically buy? If so, it might be possible to identify a tipping point at which the relationship is sufficiently mature, the firm has proved its capabilities and clients are therefore more open to use other services. There may also be a distinct pattern in the services clients buy; for example, clients who use an accountancy firm just for transfer pricing who are open to using other services, might be most likely to consider indirect tax services as their next purchase.

Through a nuanced client segmentation, it is possible to show how the same type of work can be delivered by the same firm to different types of client with very different financial outcomes. For example, a law firm may make wildly different profit margins on two similarly priced pieces of litigation where one client buyer is a CEO (and hence is relatively hands-off and so requires a short weekly update call) and one client buyer is an in-house lawyer (and hence is more involved in the detail and exchanges multiple emails and calls each day). Overlaying financial data with time-recording information also helps to assess whether the opportunity cost of non-billable time invested into winning and maintaining client relationships is proportionate to the size of the potential opportunity.

As a leader it is impossible to define a credible strategy for your firm without a distinctive understanding of where your firm makes money and which clients contribute most to profitability. Ask your finance department colleagues, as well as other practice area or team leaders in your firm, to help you compile the evidence you need. The questions below should provide a helpful starting point for your enquiries:

- Which client segments are most profitable?

- What characterizes the way the most profitable client segments interact with the firm that makes them more profitable?

- Are there clients or client types with whom the firm regularly loses money? If so, can we justify continuing to work with them for other strategic reasons?

- Which client segments are most likely to be introducers of work to other parts of your firm?

- Which client segments require the largest investment of business development and relationship management time?

- Are there any distinct patterns in the way in which clients buy services from your firm and how do these trends change as client relationships develop over time?

- What factors differentiate a profitable client engagement from an unprofitable client engagement?

In our experience the majority of firms struggle to produce client data to this level of specificity. Most firms can report client revenue fairly easily but find it more difficult to calculate profitability. Firms typically fail to apportion costs accurately, particularly when those costs are not connected to a specific project such as for sales and relationship management time. However, there are some simple steps you can take to begin to build a more accurate understanding of your costs of sale and of servicing clients and how this affects your client profitability:

- Set up and use time-recording codes for measuring the costs involved in developing and winning client opportunities and projects.

- Do likewise for activities involved with developing and managing client relationships such as client planning, project and commercial management, relationship reviews and post-project feedback.

- Look for trends in the data across different client segments and over different time periods.

- Share your findings with colleagues to see whether they can provide some narrative about their recent experiences with clients that help to explain particular trends or anomalies.

By collecting this information and sharing it with colleagues you will be able to deepen your understanding of the firm's economic model and, critically, of why certain events or trends develop in particular client relationships or client segments. Focus on the objective analysis first and then seek context – not vice versa. To make the best informed leadership decisions possible you want a dispassionate, data-led picture of your client base which can be overlaid with market analysis, internal views and client feedback.

# Understanding trends and issues in your markets

Successful leaders of professional firms maintain an outward perspective to develop a deeper understanding of the issues and trends within the various client markets in which they operate.

For Nick Holt, a former managing partner of KLegal and now a partner of SR Search, a specialist legal recruitment firm, a critical role of professional services leaders is to be aware of market changes that could represent opportunities or threats to the firm:

> As a leader in a professional firm you should be the eyes and ears of the market and have a sound understanding of the client side of things. I typically meet with our top 10 clients at least every year and have a cup of tea with the chief executive. Those conversations are obviously about relationship building but they are also a great way for me to build my understanding of the issues that matter most to our clients, where there are common issues and themes with clients and where there could be opportunities for working together that I hadn't previously thought about.

It is important to draw on external insight to validate internal views within your firm about how developments in a particular market might affect future demand for external advice. This insight should spur further thinking about whether there are opportunities to develop new service offerings to capitalize on anticipated changes in demand. For example, future changes in global tax regulations might create a need for large corporates to outsource more tax work and for a professional firm to design a technology-enabled tax management system to help clients keep track of their tax liabilities in different jurisdictions. Understanding the preparedness of clients to deal with their strategic, risk and regulatory issues in-house will give a good indication of where the strongest growth opportunities are for professional firms.

In Chapter 1 we outlined a range of external desk research sources from which to draw to build evidence in support of trend analysis. These include industry directories, client websites, analyst reports and press articles. In addition to making use of these sources, leaders should spend time having conversations with third parties and external experts who will help them to understand their markets better. These could include heads of industry associations, industry commentators and journalists, client intermediaries and introducers, and market research specialists. Use these research sources and conversations to answer the following questions:

- What factors are driving changes in client behaviour and demand?
- Are the factors shaping demand consistent across the market or are they industry-specific?
- Who is perceived to lead the market and what is their distinctive competitive advantage?
- How sustainable is the market leader's position – how easily can their competitive advantage be copied, undermined or overtaken?
- What is coming over the horizon that could catch your clients by surprise?
- In what areas are clients likely to be under-prepared and under-resourced and so will need external support?
- How concerning is the threat of new market entrants or breakthrough technologies, and what developments in a parallel market could lead to radical disruption in your area?

The answers to these questions will inform your firm's client strategy but they will also be incredibly illuminating for clients. In our experience of interviewing clients of professional firms, many find it frustrating that it is difficult to tap into the collective wisdom about market trends that exists within firms. Clients have their heads down thinking about their own business issues, so have little time for horizon scanning. As a leader you can set a positive example by playing some of these valuable market insights back to clients either through informal conversations or by identifying topics for formal marketing campaigns, press interviews or blog outputs.

The most client-focused firms have started to take an issues-led approach, rather than a service-led or sector-led approach, to describe the way that they help clients. Accountancy and advisory firm PwC, for example, lists 12 issues on its website homepage – including governance, data and analytics, risk and cyber security – that describe how their range of expertise can be deployed to address the issues facing their clients.

# Capturing feedback directly from clients

Jonathan Fox is the former managing partner of accountancy firm
Saffrey Champness. He started his career as a marketer, rising to
become head of marketing at law firm DLA Piper before taking on
executive management roles at law firm Collyer Bristow and barris-
ters set St Philips Chambers. In his experience, making time to speak
directly with clients was an incredibly valuable way to develop an
understanding of their changing needs and expectations:

> The person leading a firm has to make time available for talking to
> clients. I was the first managing partner of my firm to routinely make
> time to talk to some of our longest-standing clients. I found that even
> landed estates clients, who had been with the firm for generations, were
> changing what they needed and expected from us as their advisers.
> They expected us to change, just as they had changed. I found they were
> becoming less loyal and also being actively targeted by other firms, so
> taking time out of my schedule was important to demonstrate to our
> clients that they were highly valued and that the firm's leadership was
> listening to their views.

As Jonathan Fox suggests, rather than second guess the views of
clients, it makes sense to ask them directly about their experiences
and their future priorities, and to use these insights to influence strategic client leadership decisions. In our experience firms typically
develop through four stages of maturity when collecting and analysing feedback from clients, as illustrated in Figure 4.3. One of the main
differences between firms that progress rapidly through the stages of
the maturity curve and those that don't is the degree of leadership
buy-in and support. Firms that have strong support from leaders find
it easier to convince sceptical partners, who might be reluctant to
allow third parties to engage with their clients, about the value of
feedback. The firms with the greatest leadership buy-in also tend to
maximize response rates from clients: an introductory communication from a firm's senior partner or managing partner explaining the
purpose and value of the feedback demonstrates the seriousness and
importance of the exercise.

**Figure 4.3** The client feedback maturity curve

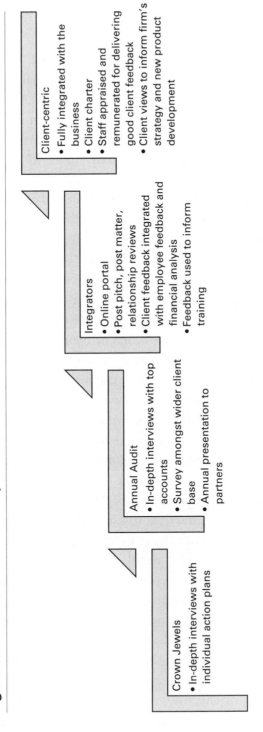

**Crown Jewels**
- In-depth interviews with individual action plans

**Annual Audit**
- In-depth interviews with top accounts
- Survey amongst wider client base
- Annual presentation to partners

**Integrators**
- Online portal
- Post pitch, post matter, relationship reviews
- Client feedback integrated with employee feedback and financial analysis
- Feedback used to inform training

**Client-centric**
- Fully integrated with the business
- Client charter
- Staff appraised and remunerated for delivering good client feedback
- Client views to inform firm's strategy and new product development

At the first level on the maturity curve – *Crown Jewels* – firms focus solely on capturing feedback from a small number of key clients, usually the top revenue generators. The insight gained is then used to create individual client action plans which detail how the firm will respond to the issues and opportunities raised in the feedback. This is a sensible place to start for firms new to capturing feedback. Although it is a cost-effective and efficient way to gather feedback, it ultimately provides only a narrow view of the client portfolio. In many firms the senior partner or managing partner is directly involved in leading some of these in-depth relationship reviews with key clients, while other firms use third parties to ensure a truly objective view of client relationships.

At the second level – *Annual Audit* – firms go one step further by incorporating key client interviews with feedback from a wider array of clients to build a more complete picture of how the firm is perceived and what are its strengths and weaknesses when working with clients. The benefit of gathering data from a wider sample of clients is that the firm's leadership can more easily identify trends over time and how performance varies between different teams within the firm. It also means that each fee-earner begins to obtain a critical mass of feedback from their own clients and so cannot easily dismiss any recurring negative feedback as being the view of a rogue dissatisfied client.

*Integrators* capture feedback from clients at different touchpoints throughout the client relationship – for example after pitches, following the addition of new clients, and after the completion of each project – and explore this insight to obtain a more comprehensive picture of the health of their client relationships. They also go beyond measuring client satisfaction to connect client feedback data with other performance indicators, for example from employee surveys or financial analysis. This enables them to build a strong business case for improving client experience by focusing on the links between client satisfaction and loyalty, fees billed and level of write-off, and to identify the amount of future revenue 'at risk' (ie from dissatisfied clients who are most at risk of defection).

Leaders of firms at this point on the maturity curve typically use the insight collected to identify a small number of firm-wide client experience priorities for improvement. They then create a strategic follow-up plan that could include skills training for fee-earners, improvements to processes and systems and client communications in order to address the areas of underperformance. Client feedback is used as the basis for leadership communications – for example at a partners' conference or in weekly firm-wide emails – to share good news stories, focus on areas for collective improvement and track progress against strategic vision.

Finally, the firms furthest ahead on the maturity curve use client feedback to accelerate their journey towards becoming truly *Client-centric*. Here there is a continuous improvement loop within the firm whereby client feedback drives behaviour change, and client feedback metrics may also be linked to performance reviews and may influence remuneration and bonuses. Our recent research among CMOs and heads of business development at professional firms indicate that although about half of firms undertake some form of regular client research, less than a quarter of firms integrate the feedback into training programmes to improve future performance or connect the feedback with other sources of client intelligence such as financial data or employee insight. However, three-quarters of firms say they have an aspiration to capture more feedback from clients over the year ahead (Beddow, 2017).

**CASE STUDY**  Using client insight at Bird & Bird to drive client service innovations

Louise Field is head of client service and insight at law firm Bird & Bird. In her role she focuses on enhancing client experience throughout the firm in order to grow and develop Bird & Bird's client relationships and keep existing clients loyal. In her view, professional firms cannot be complacent or second guess client needs, instead they need to ask clients about their experience of the firm and what they want. Insight collected at Bird & Bird has enabled the firm to pre-empt evolving client needs and shape strategic investment decisions in order to improve client experience.

So how did Louise go about collecting client insight? When she launched Client Listening at Bird & Bird Louise pledged to focus on quality of insight rather than volume of feedback activity, working with a handful of early adopters in various offices to start building a picture of what clients look for from their legal advisers and how Bird & Bird performs against these criteria. 'In my experience, most initiatives don't work if they are driven from the top downwards; it was important at the start to win people over one by one to achieve the necessary level of buy-in,' she says. With the support of the firm's senior management from the start, the Client Listening programme has steadily gained traction and has now been successfully scaled globally.

For Louise the real value of gathering feedback comes when the insight prompts change, either for one individual client, or across the board, at firm-wide level. 'Client insight has always driven strategy and change at Bird & Bird. Client Listening helps us share more Voice of the Client across more areas of the firm to inspire more of our people to build better client experiences.'

Louise's long-term aim is for clients to experience a proactive service from Bird & Bird, where tried and tested ideas are presented to new clients before they have to ask for them. 'For example, we know that clients want to see their law firms taking care of costs on their behalf, so we are working on projects to help lawyers show clients that we are planning their matters, using technology appropriately and being sensitive to their budgets,' she says.

However, change doesn't happen spontaneously. Louise supports people in Bird & Bird to use the insight collected from Client Listening interviews and surveys to understand how they might be able to work better with their clients. Importantly, after each client interview, there is a regime in place to ensure that client partners, supported by relevant business services colleagues, respond to the issues and opportunities raised and share insight with relevant colleagues. 'We also run training sessions that include listening to clients as the most effec- tive method of selling,' she says. ' We have seen time and again that just by asking questions and paying attention to the client's answers we can gather a huge amount of intelligence about what is really going on in their world and where we can help them with legal, regulatory and related consulting advice in the future.'

Bird & Bird uses client feedback to identify where to invest in developing tools that enhance client service; for example, working together with colleagues in IT, Finance and Knowledge and Learning, Louise's team has pioneered the develop- ment of tools that give clients a snapshot of progress across all their active matters globally. For Louise the speed of innovation is key: 'We enjoy being the first law firm using technology in a new way to solve a client's challenges, because that is one of the ways Bird & Bird differentiates itself against competitors.'

For firms at the vanguard of client experience measurement, client feedback is one of the sources of insight used to track progress against firm strategy. As part of their strategic vision, successful leaders within professional firms articulate client metrics, not just financial metrics, which they believe will help them measure the kind of progress the firm needs to achieve to meet its strategic ambitions. If a firm's strategy – and its potential differentiator against competitors – is to be known as having very strong sector insights among professionals at all levels throughout the firm, feedback questions should be designed to measure progress against this goal. For example, this could be as simple as the proportion of clients who rate the firm's sector expertise as 'very good' or 'outstanding', or the proportion of clients who say the firm has a reputation for having widespread expertise in a given sector.

However, it is also important to ask questions designed to help people within the firm understand the actions, attitudes and behaviours that support the client KPIs you want to measure. For example: 'What can the firm do to improve its sector expertise?' or 'How would you advise somebody in our firm to improve their understanding of issues in your sector?' These actions and behaviours can then be linked to minimum service standards or the development of a client charter that describes how you want people in your firm to engage with their clients and support skills development and capability building. Leaders who use feedback in this way move beyond feedback as a tool for understanding clients, to feedback as a tool to transform the way in which the firm works with its clients.

---

**SUMMARY**  Top tips for building a better understanding of your clients

### Analyse financial metrics at the client level, not just at a fee-earner or departmental level

As a leader it is important that you understand the true value of your client relationships and don't obsess about internally focused financial metrics such as profit per partner or practice area margin. This means capturing and reporting revenue and profitability data at a client level to understand which clients make your firm money, and the characteristics and demographics of unprofitable clients and markets. As far as possible make sure you take into account all client costs, such as relationship management time, when assessing the profitability of individual relationships.

### Segment clients to understand the characteristics of clients who contribute profit to your firm

Explore new ways of segmenting your client base such as by decision-making role, company type or length of relationship. This will help you to better understand where your firm's 'sweet spot' is – ie which client segments are high revenue/high profit and have a strong growth potential – and hence where to target your firm's client development time and effort. It may also reveal client segments that are currently unprofitable where you need to roll back your investment or refocus your approach.

### Look at a broad range of criteria when deciding which clients to prioritize

Client profitability is important but there are other factors that make a client a good fit for your firm such as cultural fit, prestige or likelihood to refer other clients. However, it is important that you understand why you plan to target particular clients or client groups if they fall into the low revenue/low profit quadrant: there must be a convincing strategic rationale for chasing opportunities with these clients.

### Capture feedback from clients to measure performance and link feedback questions to your firm's strategic client KPIs

Plot where your firm currently sits on the client feedback maturity curve, and think about the actions that will move you towards the next stage of maturity. Professional services firms should aim to conduct feedback that helps them to track progress against strategic client priorities and to improve the way that people in the firm work with clients in the future. Link the questions asked to the client service behaviours you wish to measure and improve in your firm. The more feedback you collect the clearer a view you will have about how different parts of your firm perform, where any weak links might be and what the common trends across different teams are. Don't forget to celebrate successes and positive feedback.

### Close the loop when you have collected feedback from clients

If clients give up some of their time to provide you with feedback it is because they expect to see change and action as a result. The firms that fail to act on feedback do damage to the relationship in the long-term – it suggests they haven't been listening to what the client has to say. As a leader, negative feedback should obviously be a priority: you need to ensure that teams follow through on their promises to address client concerns and that clients see an improvement in service. However, don't neglect highly satisfied clients: make sure your teams build on their efforts to win more work from these clients, capture testimonials for use in business development and invite these clients to events where they can meet with prospective clients.

# References

Beddow, Alastair (2017) Turning client service into competitive advantage, *PM Magazine*, January. Available from www.pmforum.co.uk/knowledge/ surveys/marketing-benchmark/marketing-benchmark-2017.aspx [accessed 27 March 2017]

Financial Times, Meridian West and MPF (2012) Effective client-adviser relationships, *Financial Times*. Available from: www.meridianwest. co.uk/wp-content/uploads/2015/02/relationshipStudy2012.pdf [accessed 27 March 2017]

# Connecting: how to foster a client-focused culture in your firm

05

If you look at the websites and marketing material of professional services firms you will find an abundance of phrases which suggest that everything they do revolves around their clients. 'Clients are at the heart of our business' and 'We put our clients' interests first' must be two of the most popular phrases in professional services marketing. While the sentiment behind these statements is sound, the reality is that many professional firms fail to live up to their promises of being client-centric and so the language they use to describe their firm has become devalued and undifferentiated. Client-centric has become an overused term, which, therefore, does not accurately reflect the experience many clients have when working with professional firms. In our experience only a small number of firms can stake a claim to being truly client-focused.

So, where do professional firms typically go astray in their commitment to client-centricity? Many professionals are well-intentioned, they operate with their clients' best interests at heart, and with a clear sense of duty and a service mentality. However, if you peel back the marketing veneer you will find that the way that many firms are structured, how they measure performance, reward their staff and develop ideas for new services does not support a client-focused approach. Professional firms have traditionally been very inward-looking and the language that has most currency among professionals is not at all client-focused: utilization, profits per partner, technical disciplines, charge out rates and fee-earners. It is too easy to say the right words about being client-focused without backing this up with action that delivers client-focused behaviours, organizational design and performance metrics.

In this chapter, we examine some of the building blocks that leaders need to put in place to foster a client-focused culture that helps to differentiate their firm in the mind of clients, without compromising on the value delivered back to the firm in terms of business performance or people-development opportunities. We outline how successful professional services leaders are taking steps to define client relationships more holistically in the form of a client journey and to promote opportunities for co-creation with clients.

## The building blocks of a client-focused culture

Most leaders take their firm's claim to client-focus at face value without really interrogating it further. Successful leaders spend time understanding whether their firm has the right building blocks in place to support such a claim. A client-focused culture manifests itself not just in the way that professionals deliver advice to clients but also in the way they interact with each other, how they choose to spend their time and the language they use to describe their capabilities. 'Client-focus' underpins the very fundamentals of how a professional firm is organized, develops business with its clients and trains and develops its people.

The most client-focused firms we have seen typically start by defining the client segments they wish to work for and then design systems and processes to support a focus on these segments. In practice, this means that firms with a client-focused culture:

- define a small number of high-value client segments in which they have genuine competitive advantage and can therefore 'play to win' not just 'play to compete';
- identify the needs and challenges facing potential buyers within these client segments and articulate how the firm's capabilities help clients to address their needs;
- develop personas within each client segment and map out client journeys for each persona linked to tailored value propositions (often delivered by multidisciplinary teams);

- allocate the majority of their marketing and business development (BD) resources to client segments, not to practice areas or technical disciplines;

- allocate BD personnel to each client segment – often these might be specialists with relevant industry knowledge or experience who can offer proactive support to fee-earners;

- tailor their website and other marketing information with relevant messages, imagery and content that will help clients to self-identify as a prospective client of the firm;

- have an organizational design and leadership structure that aligns with client segments; and

- develop individual appraisal and evaluation metrics that highlight contribution to client segments, including cross-referrals from within the firm.

If that seems a long-way off, a helpful place to start is to ask yourself the following open question: what do we see in our firm that supports, and doesn't support, a truly client-focused culture? Ask others in your firm for their ideas and identify where there are shared concepts and divergent points of view. If you are feeling brave you can even ask clients directly because their unvarnished opinions are helpful for identifying instances where the rhetoric used does not quite tally with their direct experience. We have used this question as the basis for interactive exercises with many professional firms and their clients, with some of the most commonly cited responses outlined in Figure 5.1.

Commonly cited building blocks supporting a client-focused culture include:

- a professional culture in which clients and employees are treated with respect and their contribution to the firm is recognized by colleagues and peers;

- a passion for client advocacy, where people get under the skin of the strategic, personal and business goals of clients to truly understand their motivations and desired outcomes;

- a client relationship management programme, in which relationships are formalized, regularly reviewed and client needs and interests are proactively identified;

**Figure 5.1**    The building blocks that support, or don't support, a client-focused culture

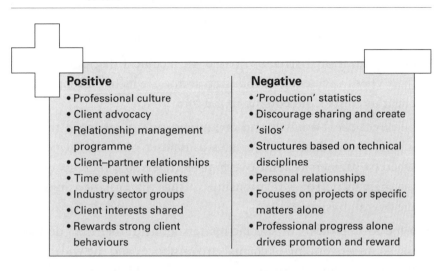

| Positive | Negative |
|---|---|
| • Professional culture | • 'Production' statistics |
| • Client advocacy | • Discourage sharing and create 'silos' |
| • Relationship management programme | • Structures based on technical disciplines |
| • Client–partner relationships | • Personal relationships |
| • Time spent with clients | • Focuses on projects or specific matters alone |
| • Industry sector groups | • Professional progress alone drives promotion and reward |
| • Client interests shared | |
| • Rewards strong client behaviours | |

- mutually beneficial client–partner relationships, in which the interests of clients and the firm are properly aligned;

- a regular investment in spending time with clients through conversations, meetings, secondments, and client visits (client-focused firms do this proactively without being asked);

- formal and informal groups focused on industry sector or client segments to identify common trends and issues facing clients, and to repurpose these insights to deliver greater value to clients;

- sharing and discussion of client interests across the firm, or within teams, to find ways to collaborate better to meet the changing needs of clients; and

- a leadership that communicates, celebrates and rewards strong client behaviours, not just billable hours or profitability.

Commonly cited building blocks that don't support a client-focused culture include:

- performance measures focused primarily on 'production statistics' such as utilization, billable hours and charge out rates, rather than client value delivered, or client satisfaction;

- a leadership that incentivizes behaviours that discourage the sharing of information and creation of silos by not rewarding collaboration, or by linking performance directly to a practice area P&L rather than financial performance by client segment;

- an organizational structure based on technical disciplines rather than client segments or industry sectors, which prevent shared client interests from coming to the fore;

- all direct client content and communication is managed through a single individual – this creates a mindset of client 'ownership' whereby partners become overly protective about their clients and see them as personal relationships, rather than relationships with the overall business;

- a focus on projects or specific matters alone, rather than developing an understanding of clients' circumstances and the wider issues the firm's technical capabilities can help to address;

- professional progress alone drives promotion and reward, rather than a balanced scorecard of client development and people development measures.

As you can see from the examples listed above, strong leadership plays a vital role in defining and implementing the building blocks of a client-focused culture in any professional services firm. As a leader you need to build client-focus into your strategic vision, defining what it means in the context of the kinds of clients you work with and the markets in which your firm operates. You need to communicate clearly which principles of client-focus apply consistently across interactions with all clients and which can be flexed to adapt to the specific characteristics of different client segments. For example, being client-focused with public sector clients means something different (such as being conscious of budgetary pressures or resource shortage for non-critical projects) from being client-focused with wealthy entrepreneur clients (such as proactively bringing business-growth opportunities and possible acquisition targets).

Asking yourself, your colleagues and your clients to what extent your firm is currently client-focused may reveal some difficult home truths. However, it will also reveal helpful insights from which you can begin to make changes to move your firm towards becoming more genuinely client-focused. As you start to build a plan for addressing the opportunities and challenges highlighted, you might find the following questions helpful to guide your thinking:

- How do you reinforce and celebrate the positives you have identified? Is there anything you, your team or the firm collectively can do to hardwire these behaviours into your culture?

- Who are the role models for great client-focused behaviour that you can champion? How do you shine a light on their behaviour and encourage others to follow their lead?

- Why have the negatives developed in the way they have? What is the root cause?

- Is there a consensus view on the negatives identified? What is the impact of these negative behaviours or activities on the client experience?

- How do you shift the balance away from the negative towards positive client-focused attributes?

- Even if you cannot unpick a central plank of your firm's culture, is there a counter-weight you can introduce to offset the negative attributes? For example, rather than jettisoning internal production measures entirely, you may want to move to a balanced scorecard approach to measuring the firm's performance, which includes a range of client-focused metrics.

Other sections of this handbook will help you to address some of the specific issues you uncover as part of your initial client-focus assessment. The rest of this chapter explores ways that you, as a leader, can begin to move your firm towards becoming more client-focused.

## Improve the client experience and mapping the client journey

Traditionally, professional firms conceptualized their relationships with clients as a series of disparate touch-points moving from pitching for work, through winning work and delivering work, to maintaining the relationship. In this model, clients engaged with professional firms to solve specific issues or to buy a specific service, and over time this may have resulted in a recurring relationship and new opportunities to work together. That thinking is too simplistic because it fails to take account of the importance for clients of the experiential nature of working with professional firms. At a time when technical advice is no longer a true differentiator for professionals, the quality of client experience – how it feels to be a client of a particular firm – can make or break a client relationship.

Client experience may sound 'fluffy', but it is not a nebulous concept. Clients and prospective clients continually make judgements about professional firms to assess whether it is the type of organization they want to work with, whether they will work well together with the people they meet, and whether they identify a cultural and experiential fit. Some of these judgements will be based on matter-related experiences, but many won't; experiences such as seeing a partner giving a presentation at a conference, interacting with staff on a firm's reception desk or visiting a firm's website all influence how people perceive a firm and evaluate their possible fit with that firm.

Our research among clients of professional firms shows that there is a direct correlation between how clients rate the quality of the experience they have, working with their professional advisers, and the extent to which they intend to remain loyal to that firm in the future. Superior client experience, therefore, solidifies the relationship by making it very difficult for clients to find a reason to defect to a competitor. Client-focused firms understand this and their leaders take steps to ensure that their client experience is consistent and seamless no matter which department, in which office, or through which channel, the client interacts with the firm.

One way for leaders to understand the holistic client experience in their firm is to create a client journey map. This is a process that charts the typical client engagement from initial marketing to project close, highlighting the moments that matter most to clients and where there are opportunities to work more efficiently. Rather than focus only on discrete touch-points, a journey map also highlights how clients move from one stage of their relationship with a firm to another: typically this involves handovers between team members where information can be lost or miscommunicated. These experiential gaps between touch-points are often a cause of major client dissatisfaction.

Customer-focused organizations such as retail, Technology, Media and Telecommunications (TMT) and consumer goods companies have been thinking about customer relationships in this way for a long time, but the principles of journey mapping have only recently been applied within professional services firms. Research we have undertaken among CMOs and heads of business development in professional firms shows that almost half (48 per cent) plan to create a client journey map within the next 12 months, and that 23 per cent plan to develop a client charter that sets out the firm's service promise to clients at different points on the client journey (Beddow, 2017).

As a leader, you will find that a client journey map is a helpful tool for promoting client-focused behaviours. It gives you a framework you can use to champion client-focused behaviour and to encourage people in your firm to think more widely about client experience and how their interactions shape client perceptions of the firm. As the case study below illustrates, creating a client journey map is a collaborative exercise, which involves synthesizing the views of people within a firm and of the clients themselves. Asking clients how they would like your firm to work with them can be incredibly eye-opening and empowering for clients and can help to cement the relationship by identifying practical and replicable ways of working better, and more consistently, together in future.

**CASE STUDY**   Mapping the client journey to improve client experience at Grant Thornton International

Grant Thornton International Ltd (GTIL)* is a \$4.8 billion international network of independent audit, tax and advisory firms with 47,000 staff across 130 different countries. In developing the new 2020 global strategy, differentiation was a key consideration, which in turn led to a strategic focus on the brand experience for

*Grant Thornton International Ltd (GTIL) and its member firms are not a worldwide partnership. GTIL and each member firm are separate legal entities. Services are delivered by the member firms. GTIL does not provide services to clients. GTIL and its member firms are not agents of, and do not obligate, one another and are not liable for one another's acts or omissions.

clients, employees and wider communities. As Prity Kanjia, GTIL's Global Client Experience Programme Manager, explains, the firm saw the Grant Thornton experience and financial performance as intrinsically linked: 'We came to an understanding that if the firm creates a fantastic experience internally for its people, then that will create a fantastic experience for our clients. With a fantastic client experience, growth in revenue will follow.'

With a new strategic goal in place, GTIL set about implementing the actions that would support the delivery of an outstanding client experience. Its first area of focus was client feedback. At the time, GTIL had no consistent mechanism for reporting client feedback and there was no mandate for member firms to collect such data. The firm needed a baseline from which to judge improvements in client experience, so GTIL's Board of Governors agreed that all member firms should measure client feedback by the end of 2016.

However, simply collecting feedback wasn't enough to drive change; this insight had to be linked back to the firm's overall growth strategy. A key part of GTIL's strategy is to win more multinational work from large corporates but this meant being able to offer a consistent client experience for clients engaging with multiple Grant Thornton member firms across the world. As Prity explains: 'It is important for us to reassure multinationals that they will get the same level of experience across all our markets, regardless of how we work behind the scenes.'

To address inconsistencies in the client experience, GTIL first appointed a team of client experience champions in each member firm to act as evangelists who would promote the benefits of improving client experience to their colleagues. Next the firm set about developing a client journey map. This framework visualizes what a typical Grant Thornton client might experience when working with a member firm/s, including how they select providers, how the service is delivered to them and how the relationship evolves over time. By mapping out client interactions in this way, Grant Thornton wanted to understand better where clients might have suboptimal experiences and where there were opportunities to add more value to clients.

With a draft framework in place, GTIL – with the help of consultancy Meridian West – carried out in-depth interviews with partners from member firms around the world to validate the framework and to identify examples of good practice behaviours at each stage of the journey that could be replicated in other parts of the world. The internal reactions were overwhelmingly positive. A sample group of clients was then also interviewed to understand which parts of the journey they thought added most value to their experience of working with external auditors and business advisers. Using these internal and external insights, GTIL defined minimum service standards for each step of the client journey. These were supported with a number of 'brilliant basics' – the simple things that have a disproportionate impact on client experience – as well as advanced practice techniques that would stretch member firms that were already delivering high levels of client service.

The next step for GTIL is to use its client journey map and client experience behaviours as part of its global learning and development programmes. The firm is developing a series of workshops that will focus on improving the client experience capabilities of Grant Thornton staff around the world. These will include a particular focus on training for new staff to make sure they adopt good customer service habits from the outset of their career. The firm will continue to collect client feedback at the different stages of the client journey in order to track improvements as a result of its implementation programme.

In Prity's view mapping the client journey has had many benefits. 'We have identified opportunities to introduce more efficient project management and improve our global coordination, both of which should lead to better margins and increase the likelihood of gaining repeat work from our clients,' she says. GTIL has developed a better understanding of how clients come to work with member firms in the first place, and is now better able to pinpoint exactly where clients are most at risk of defection. 'Once you become known as a firm that delivers excellent client service,' says Prity, 'people want to work with you again and again. They give you more work, they recommend you to their colleagues and peers, and that leads to business growth.'

Although a client journey map is a fairly tactical exercise to undertake, it has many strategic benefits for leaders wanting to improve client-focus in their firms. Five of the main strategic client leadership benefits are outlined below:

**1 A deeper understanding of the needs of different client segments**

Client journey maps highlight the human aspect of the client experience and the emotional and experiential elements of working with professional firms. The process treats clients as individuals not organizations, and in doing so helps a firm to gain a better understanding of the motivations of different client segments; how the way the firm works with clients can be aligned to these motivations.

**2 A greater focus on the moments that matter and prioritization of resource**

Professional firms are notoriously bad at over-servicing their clients, providing a Rolls Royce service when a client expects, and wants to pay for, a Ford Escort. Mapping out the client journey identifies the moments that matter most to clients and so budgets, time and people resources can be prioritized accordingly.

**3 Clearly articulated client experience best practice, which can be used to support training and development**

A client journey map should be underpinned by a useful bank of best practice examples, templates and behaviours that bring the map to life and show to people what they need to do to delight clients at each stage of the client journey. This in turn creates a useful resource for tailored skills training, coaching and other people-development initiatives.

**4 Reducing inefficiency in client experience to increase financial performance**

Mapping the different processes involved in meeting client needs at, and between, multiple touch-points on the client journey, can help to identify opportunities for standardizations and greater efficiency. Professional firms typically over-engineer the way they work with clients and spend unrecoverable time reinventing processes without due cause. Most service methodologies (tax advice, audit, disputes, property management, etc) can be distilled into repeatable processes that can usually be simplified or streamlined further.

**5 An evidence-based message about what makes a firm different from competitors**

As a leader, you can use the journey map as a framework for measuring performance at moments of the client experience that are most important for clients. One way of doing this is to create a series of minimum service standards that you expect everybody in the firm to deliver when engaging with clients and with their colleagues. When you have built internal commitment to deliver against these service standards they can be articulated to the external market to highlight how your firm is different from its competitors. Examples used by firms include a client service charter, minimum service standards in pitches and tender documents, and client experience differentiators in other marketing materials.

# The role of the client champion in fostering a client-focused culture

Given the importance of delivering consistently excellent client experience to the success of professional firms, it is disappointing that our research among CMOs and heads of business development in professional services firms suggests that less than a quarter (just 21 per cent) of firms directly measure and reward performance based on the quality of client experience delivered. However, as we outlined in Chapter 4 of this handbook, more firms are beginning to use client feedback as a mechanism for directly measuring aspects of the client experience, and to link this to how performance is measured and rewarded (Beddow, 2017).

One strategy that some leaders are using to establish a client-focused culture is to nominate and promote client champions within their firm. These are individuals who are widely regarded as delivering a consistently high level of client experience, who go 'above and beyond' for clients, and who can inspire others in the firm to replicate their success. We explored the role of client champions in detail in a previous publication, where we identified six attributes (Clark and Nixon, 2015). These are described in Figure 5.2.

A client champion is somebody who:

- understands the client's goals as well as the client does themselves;
- tracks trends and market developments relevant to the client and shares this information proactively with the client and within their own team;
- can advise the client on a range of issues, irrespective of technical capability – they are first and foremost known as a great adviser to the client, not a consultant or lawyer or accountant;

- builds deep networks in the client organization from top to bottom, including building relationships with the client's wider group of business advisers;

- gets and takes the call from the principal client contact whenever they have a serious business issue to discuss, regardless of the specific technical capability to which that issue may apply; and

- understands the wider value their firm can add to the client and introduces the right person at the right time to help the client address a known or unknown need.

It is also important for you as a leader to set expectations in your firm about what a client champion is not. A client champion is not somebody who will simply bend over backwards and always give in to client demands. That is a lapdog, not a client champion. Any true client champion knows it is important to be strong and, where necessary, challenge perceived wisdom in the client organization. True client champions are able to create relationships that work for the best interests of the client, as well as for the firm and its people; they know when to make trade-offs and concessions and when to

**Figure 5.2**   Six attributes of a client champion

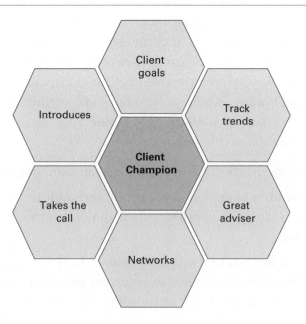

stand their ground. In the next chapter of this handbook we will turn our attention to effective client relationship management (CRM) and some of the links between client leadership, client champions and effective CRM.

In our experience client champions don't just have to be partners; some of the most effective client champions we have come across have been associates or relatively junior fee-earners who are able intuitively to place themselves in their clients' shoes and anticipate how the needs of clients are evolving. Whoever your client champions are, they will have valuable insights that others in the firm can learn from and it is important to encourage them to share these experiences with others. Find ways to capture these insights such as in videos, at town hall meetings and on team awaydays and share them with colleagues.

## Co-create solutions with clients

Client champions are often natural collaborators. They understand that working with clients involves a two-way relationship and they use their network to bring the best people to the table – both from within the firm and within the client's organization – to address a particular issue or opportunity. At the heart of effective co-creation is keeping the client front of mind and keeping eyes open to potential opportunities for collaboration. In a competitive market you need to work out the best way of sustaining the relationships you have with clients, and to make sure that your firm is always front of mind for each one. In today's market the risk of displacement is much greater than it has ever been, particularly with new types of entrant emerging. Sticking like glue to your clients will almost certainly require your firm to be much more flexible in the way that it works with clients in future. That might mean coaching your professionals to take on the mindset of a consultant, not just a technical adviser. It could also mean finding the external partners you need to collaborate with in order to deliver new types of service to clients.

Professionals have long been encouraged to aspire to the role of the 'trusted adviser'. However, some professionals have taken this to mean that clients want to outsource all of their thinking to their adviser, whom they will trust to come up with solutions on their behalf. In most instances clients are not looking for such a one-sided relationship. They see a 'trusted adviser' as somebody who they can share ideas with, use as a sounding board for challenges and trust to understand the bigger picture. In essence they want somebody that they can collaborate with to co-create solutions that produce the best outcome possible for their particular situation.

In a truly collaborative relationship, the client and the professional share in the identification, solution and resolution of a situation or project. The two individuals or organizations work in partnership, sharing resources, risks and rewards. This works both ways: clients and professionals work together to solve client issues and to help firms to test out new ideas for services, refine new propositions and improve the way they work together. Law firm Addleshaw Goddard, for example, launched its Client Development Centre in 2005, through which it collaborates with its clients to address some of the wider organizational challenges, not just legal problems, through the delivery of bespoke advice, consultancy and training. A key tenet of the programme is for Addleshaw Goddard to work with General Counsel clients to co-create solutions that enhance the reputation and effectiveness of clients within their own organization.

As a leader it is important that you make the case for the benefits of co-creation with clients. You need to communicate the message that effective co-creation starts with open, collaborative conversations with clients and a deep understanding of the client's business. Gareth Mason has held CEO roles in three legal practices. In his view, collaborative conversations with clients – ideally on the client's premises – are a great way to get professionals to understand their clients' businesses properly:

One idea that I have seen work really well in the past is reverse seminars. Invite clients to host seminars talking about their own business, but run these as a conversation not simply a one-way presentation. Encourage your team to ask questions and get enthused. It is even better if these seminars can be held at the client's premises so that your team can have a walk around the factory or office and meet a few other people as well, taking the opportunity to have a look behind the scenes and really get under the skin of how the client's business works.

The firms that are able to build collaborative solutions with their clients will be better equipped to seek out opportunities to differentiate how they work with clients, deliver measurable value to clients' businesses and build new business models that break away from the traditional hourly rate. Effective co-creation can bring about projects that bind a firm and its client together for the long term. It can also support collaborative working between teams within a firm; later on in Chapter 8 of this handbook we will explore in depth how great people leaders drive high performance in their teams by fostering greater collaboration internally.

In our experience, the most client-focused firms have co-creation in their DNA. However, we have also seen at first-hand that co-creation is a relatively new concept for professionals, many of whom struggle to put it into practice. Figure 5.3 outlines five simple steps to fostering greater co-creation as part of your firm's client-focused culture. This builds on the approach to innovation described in Chapter 2 of this handbook.

Like innovation, co-creation is an open process. Finding mutually-beneficial solutions to shared problems requires experimentation and repetition within set parameters, what we referred to as the 'Innovation Sandbox' in Chapter 2. An idea does not need to be

**Figure 5.3**    A five-step process for co-creating with clients

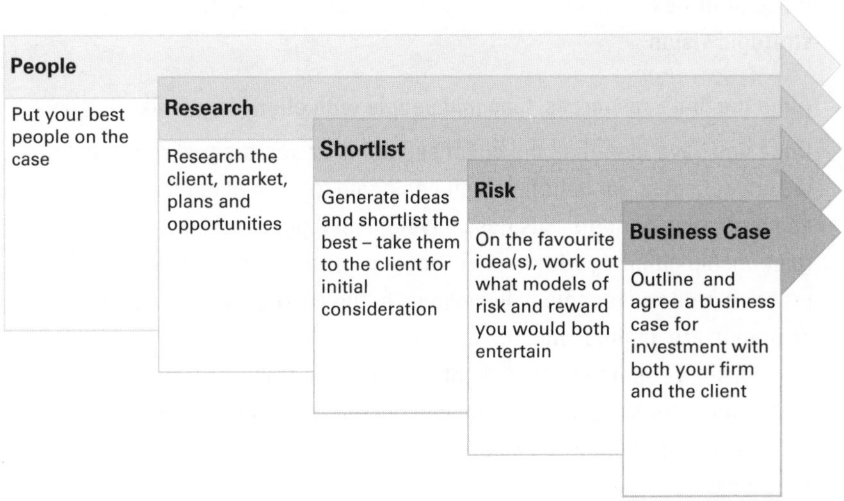

**People**
Put your best people on the case

**Research**
Research the client, market, plans and opportunities

**Shortlist**
Generate ideas and shortlist the best – take them to the client for initial consideration

**Risk**
On the favourite idea(s), work out what models of risk and reward you would both entertain

**Business Case**
Outline and agree a business case for investment with both your firm and the client

perfect before it can be shared with a client; considered options and possible solutions are usually sufficient to spark dialogue about further refinements needed. This 'good enough' mentality at the heart of co-creation can be challenging at first for professionals who are used to always knowing a right answer and demonstrating their mastery to clients. One way to reduce the risk of co-creation and free up people's thinking, is to consider potential collaboration projects as pilots, whereby the firm will commit time and resource over a limited period before evaluating whether or not to continue the project. Any perceived damaging consequence of failure is therefore minimized.

---

**SUMMARY**  Top tips for establishing a client-focused culture in your firm

### Use client insight to help you identify the building blocks in your firm that don't support a client-focused culture

Test whether your firm's actions, organizational design and incentives support a client-focused culture or not. It is helpful to gather opinions from within the firm but also to speak to clients to identify where there are gaps between internal views and the external reality experienced by clients. Create a plan for turning negative factors into positive building blocks to foster a client-focused culture, and then communicate these priorities within the firm as part of your client leadership and strategic vision.

### Align the firm's resources, time and people with client segments

Once you have identified the client segments or sectors that represent the 'sweet spots' for your firm, you can begin to align client development and marketing budgets, business development, personnel and relationship planning with these client segments rather than with practice areas or technical disciplines. In the most client-focused firms, all people are aligned with one or more client segments. This helps to share insights about specific client segments internally, promotes a better understanding of the technical capabilities of colleagues who service similar client types so that opportunities for collaboration can be more easily spotted.

### Map the client journey, and give teams ownership of client journeys within their own domain

Understand how clients experience working with your firm at a logical and an emotional level and how they feel at various touch-points along this journey. Identify which touch-points matter most to clients and prioritize time and resources accordingly, but don't forget to focus on what happens in between various touch-points because poor communication and ineffective handovers are often a cause of major dissatisfaction and poor client experience. With a firm-wide journey map in place you can identify consistent, minimum service standards for client experience, and then cascade the firm-wide journey map to individual delivery teams for them to adapt to their own way of working with clients, within the parameters set by the minimum service standards.

### Capture internal best practice and share the wisdom of client champions within the firm

Identify the individuals that really have the clients' interests at heart and encourage wider use of the client-focused behaviour they display. Encourage them to set an example for others and, as a leader, you should put their client leadership characteristics on the highest pedestal. Using a framework such as a journey map, capture best practices used by client champions and share these examples with others in the firm: ask champions to prepare short videos about how they handle different client service scenarios to show others the best way to improve their own performance.

### Embrace the opportunity to co-create solutions with clients

Sit down with your best clients and look for mutually beneficial opportunities to solve client issues and improve the firm's service propositions. Don't let the prevailing operating model, or natural conservatism, of your firm get in the way. Co-creating solutions will involve finding an appropriate balance of investment, reward and risk. As a leader, it is important that you also give people the freedom and space to test and develop solutions that might not be perfect first time around. Develop a consultative and client-focused mindset within your firm by encouraging people to see issues from the client's perspective and then to ask clients open questions to identify where there is an opportunity to work together to create solutions.

# References

Beddow, Alastair (2017) Turning client focus into competitive advantage,
   *PM Magazine*, January 2017. Available from: www.pmforum.co.uk/
   knowledge/surveys/marketing-benchmark/marketing-benchmark-2017.
   aspx [accessed 02 March 2017]
Clark, Nigel and Nixon, Charles (2015) *Professional Services Marketing
   Handbook*, Kogan Page, London

# Sales: how to improve your firm's client-development success 06

Many professionals recoil from the word 'sales'. A reluctance to recognize the importance of selling as an essential skill in the professional's toolkit is an anachronism from an earlier age when professional services firms were restricted from marketing, let alone actively selling, their services. Nonetheless, the need to sell (even if it is called business development or client relationship management) is never far from the top of a professional's to-do list in this age of disruption. With a more diverse ecosystem of possible competitors operating within the professional services market, professionals cannot become complacent about the need to sell themselves and their firm to potential clients.

What professionals do not always take time to consider, however, is the most productive way for them to win work. In professional firms, the biggest expense involved in winning work is not typically the out-of-pocket cost of business development team salaries, marketing campaigns and events but the time costs associated with having senior professionals spending many hours of their time on unfocused sales and client development activity. Every hour spent on non-chargeable work is an hour's worth of income that a professional forgoes, so it is important that business development time is spent on activities that have the best possible chance of generating future business and not on displacement activity. It is not uncommon to find the opportunity cost of time spent on business development to be many multiples of – often more than 10 times – the cash outlay.

In earlier chapters we explored the best way for leaders to focus their firm's efforts on the right kind of opportunities so that time is not squandered pursuing clients that will contribute to low profitability for the firm. However, while it is important to define the 'sweet spot' in the market where a professional firm can differentiate and 'play to win', it is equally important to define the kind of activities that will contribute to sales, or what we call client development success.

In this chapter we focus on the strategies leaders of professional services firms can use to maximize sales success throughout their firm, so that, rather than rely on a small number of rainmakers, leaders develop a culture that promotes and develops the skills and approaches needed to win work from their desired clients. This encompasses client relationship management, as well as sales pipeline and business development strategies.

## Client relationship management underpins effective client development

Effective client development starts by creating long-term, sustainable client relationships based on mutual understanding of agreed outcomes and objectives. It is far easier to nurture and grow existing client relationships to generate recurring work, or introduce new services to existing clients, than it is to continually find new clients to whom a firm must sell afresh. In the previous two chapters we highlighted the importance of understanding and anticipating how client needs are evolving and of creating collaborative and trusted relationships with clients. Both of these activities are essential foundations of effective client development and generate powerful insight about clients that feed into any client relationship management programme. A structured process around client development can make the sales and business development process far more efficient with much less time wasted chasing fruitless opportunities even for professional firms whose business model is more transactional.

Although client relationship management (CRM) is a familiar process to most professional services firms, the phrase is most often associated with unloved technology systems, which require professionals to keep all their client information, contact details and meeting records in a database. The intrinsic value of the system is only high if records are comprehensive and kept up to date. Although technology is usually an important component of a successful CRM process, it is not the heart of it. At the core of effective CRM is an ethos, discipline and set of behaviours around client development that demonstrate how a firm prioritizes, invests in, manages and develops its relationships with clients and prospective clients. While the vast majority of firms have specialist business development professionals who can advise on and support the development of a CRM process, leaders of professional firms need to set a vision for the kind of relationships the firm wants to have with its clients and set expectations about how colleagues should spend their client development time.

One of the biggest traps that professional firms fall into with CRM is trying to manage all relationships to the same high standard. Leaders should set minimum standards about the service levels and relationship development commitment that all clients of a firm can expect, but they need to be clear that it is not an appropriate use of time and resources to give gold-plated service to clients who generate small fees and represent limited growth potential. In Chapters 1 and 4 of this handbook we explored the concept of identifying a firm's 'sweet spot' and, as a general rule, client development resources and efforts should be prioritized here, together with long-standing clients who are strategically important for the continued success of the firm. To help plan and prioritize client relationship management activity, it is helpful to think in terms of five building blocks for an effective CRM approach as outlined in Figure 6.1 below.

**Figure 6.1**  Five client relationship management essentials

In our experience the most effective CRM approaches should:

- **Have a clear focus on a defined group of priority clients**

  There should be recognition across the business which clients are included in any client development initiative and why. Those clients should know they are on the programme and understand what the benefits are to them. As a leader you need to watch out for people spending too much time with low revenue/low profitability clients, which have limited growth potential, and point out examples of poor prioritization. Firms should apply the same rigorous principles to developing their relationships with other market participants such as intermediaries and third party collaborators who are important for generating work. The concept of reciprocity is likely to be important in sustaining long-term, trusted relationships with these individuals.

- **Give clear, delegated responsibility to partners and other senior fee-earners**

  High value client relationships need somebody to lead their development. This shouldn't be allowed to develop organically or without direction: in most firms this will be a senior fee-earner – usually referred to as a client relationship partner or director – although some firms have dedicated client relationship roles that are undertaken by specialist business development professionals, or the role is assigned to associates, managers or other individuals on the track to partnership. A client relationship partner is responsible for getting under the skin of the client's business and personal objectives, identifying potential opportunities and taking the whole firm to the client so that the client is aware of the many possible ways the firm can help them in the future. This person usually becomes the 'go to' person in the client's mind whenever they have an issue or want to discuss an opportunity, even if they are not ultimately responsible for overseeing the delivery of work.

- **Be supported by a well-informed and well-coordinated team**

  To be effective in their role, client relationship partners should be encouraged to share insights and opportunities, gained from their conversations with clients, among the rest of the team in the firm, and to introduce relevant colleagues proactively to the client. Openness, collaboration and encouragement are the watchwords of an effective client relationship partner. This creates a 'zippered' relationship – in which there are many points of interlinking contact – rather than a relationship dependent on a single, point-to-point contact. It is the relationship partner's role to ensure the team is briefed and well-coordinated, and to organize regular face-to-face time to discuss new opportunities.

- **Be underpinned with a plan of activity to grow the relationship**

  All priority clients should have a client development plan that details the long-term, strategic objectives for the development of the relationship, along with short-term activities to maintain ongoing contact. This could include events that the client will be invited to, regular insights that will be shared with the client and when and how the relationship will be formally reviewed. Ideally, this plan should be shared with, and developed in collaboration with, the client, and supported by regular meetings with the client led by the client relationship partner and attended by others in the firm who work with the client. Although it is important that client development priorities and initiatives are documented and shared, as a leader you want to avoid the planning process being too onerous so that people spend the majority of their time in conversation with clients rather than behind their desks planning.

- **Link with how performance is measured and reward client-focused behaviours**

  It is important that a firm's reward and recognition structures align with its client development priorities. Achieving agreed actions on a client development plan should be a reason for rewarding professionals and a contributing factor to their career progression. It is important that leaders recognize client-focused behaviours in the whole client team, not just in client relationship partners. Although it might not always be possible to link remuneration directly with client development activity, some firms have had success motivating their teams by celebrating and rewarding client-focused behaviours with small but meaningful rewards such as bottles of champagne or retail vouchers.

When done well, client relationship management provides a solid foundation on which firms can build a more client-focused culture. In the firms that do this well, client development becomes an integral part of the firm's core ethos and developing relationships with clients is recognized as the collective responsibility of everybody in the firm, no matter what their level of seniority.

As Joanna Worby, managing partner of law firm Brachers points out, it is important that people are given responsibility, but are also made accountable, for developing client relationships throughout their professional careers:

> In my experience it is important to make individuals accountable for their relationships with clients as early as possible in their career. We expect our professionals to take responsibility for managing the development of certain client relationships and to have a client care plan in place for how they intend to look after and grow the client relationship. When people have their regular catch-up meetings with colleagues in the firm, we expect people to keep track of how frequently we have met with the client and whether there are new opportunities arising. When you make people accountable, however, it is vital to celebrate successes: when we receive good feedback from a client we openly acknowledge it within the team and across the firm. People like the accolade and deserve the reward and it motivates them to keep doing a good job.

In addition to the formal, structured side of client relationship management, there are a number of informal things you can do as a leader to support and reinforce the success of your firm's client development programme. Don't underestimate the impact of showing an interest in the client relationships your colleagues are developing, asking them questions about the opportunities they are pursuing and proactively sharing insights and ideas about possible opportunities. Set aside time to get involved in client relationship reviews or to attend internal team planning meetings for strategically important clients for the firm. These small investments of time demonstrate to people that the firm's leaders treat client development seriously and they should do too.

## Maximize success across the sales pipeline

As a leader you need to make sure you have the right processes, management expertise and client leadership in place to deliver a steady stream of profitable sales. One of the most common ways that professional firms track their client development activity is through a

**Figure 6.2**  The sales pipeline

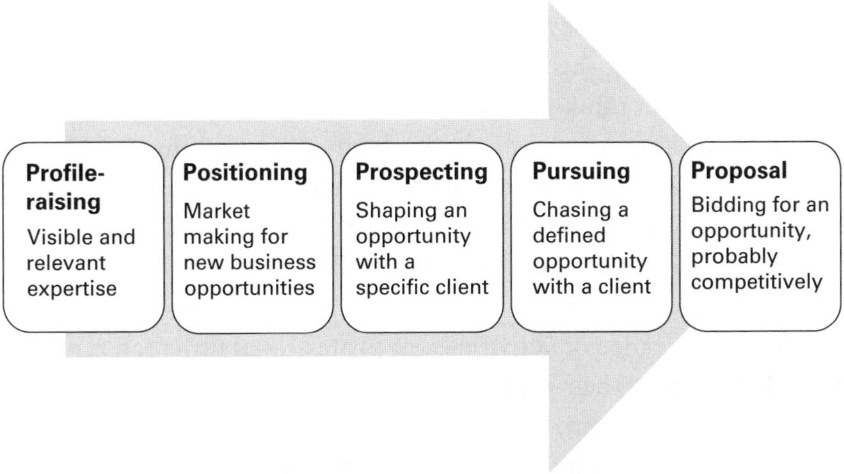

| Profile-raising | Positioning | Prospecting | Pursuing | Proposal |
|---|---|---|---|---|
| Visible and relevant expertise | Market making for new business opportunities | Shaping an opportunity with a specific client | Chasing a defined opportunity with a client | Bidding for an opportunity, probably competitively |

sales pipeline, five core elements of which are outlined in Figure 6.2. New opportunities appear at the top of the sales pipeline and flow through to generate work at the end of the pipeline. Of course, sales pipelines are leaky and porous, and opportunities will enter and exit at different points and move at variable speeds.

Winning the right work from the right clients is in large part about progressing opportunities in the pipeline at an appropriate speed, pushing out those that you don't want and focusing maximum time and attention on those that really matter. As a leader, one of the critical roles you can play is to ensure priority client opportunities receive the constant and deliberate attention they require. Managing this process successfully requires leaders to be ruthlessly objective about the potential chances of success for any given opportunity, cutting losses and weeding out weak opportunities in order to invest time and energy in fewer, but better opportunities. Successful leaders actively decide what they want to win, not just what they cannot afford to lose.

## Sales pipeline: profile-raising

Profile-raising is the first element of a healthy sales pipeline because without building awareness in the market it is very difficult for a firm to be high enough on a client's consideration list when the client identifies a need to seek external advice. Market profile is also intrinsically linked to a professional firm's brand identity, which describes what the client experiences when working with a firm and how that is different from competitors. Professionals obsess about their profiles – how well they think they are known and regarded in their market and among their peers – but too often they focus on raising visibility without thinking about the relevant audience they are trying to target. It is important to think about profile-raising as building visible and relevant expertise in the market. This is an important way to avoid expensive vanity projects that raise profiles indiscriminately and so don't often generate a substantial pipeline of quality opportunities.

There are a range of activities that professional firms can typically introduce to raise their profile among clients, from speaking at external conferences to producing marketing publications and running their own events. Each of these has potential value but is only worthwhile if the investment of time and money needed to bring it about will generate a sufficient return in terms of moving people through a pipeline towards an eventual sale. When assessing what activities your firm could arrange to raise its profile, you should find it helpful to think through answers to the following questions:

- Audience: what is the target audience with whom we want to raise profile and how diverse is that audience?

- Baseline: do we have a clear, objective baseline of our current market profile with our target audience? How does this audience perceive us compared to our competitors?

- Value: how important is market profile to our target audience when they make a decision about which firms to work with?

- Investment: how much investment of time and money is required to achieve the anticipated benefit? To what extent will the activity raise visibility within the target audience and reinforce our firm's brand?

- Impact: how will we measure or quantify the return on investment? Can we place an objective value on the benefit gained or will we have to rely on a subjective assessment?

- Review: how will we review the impact after the event to understand lessons for improving future profile-raising activity?

The more a firm is able to review the impact of the profile-raising initiatives, the better their judgement will be on the effectiveness of future potential investments.

## Sales pipeline: positioning

Once a client is aware of a professional firm, the next threshold to be crossed is for the client to believe that the firm is the right kind of organization to help them with their challenges and with whom they could actively picture themselves working. We call this positioning because it is about aligning the client's and the firm's capabilities and interests to create a viable relationship. Positioning is often an area in which we find leaders of professional firms chronically under-invest, because it requires deep client and market understanding, foresight and imagination. Short-sighted leaders believe that awareness and a solid market reputation are sufficient for their firm to pass the positioning test, but very few clients will buy off reputation alone.

Positioning requires firms to think about how the services and capabilities that they offer can best be aligned with the changing needs and requirements of their clients and markets, in such a way that the firm has a compelling story to tell to the market. Doing this successfully often depends on connecting teams of professionals from different disciplines to develop multidisciplinary perspectives on market or client challenges. It is very hard to do this without a deep understanding of the issues likely to be top of the agenda for clients over the coming months and years; reaching this deep level of understanding requires some investment of time and effort to ask exploratory questions of clients about their future business needs.

As a leader, you can make a real difference to the seriousness with which your firm takes positioning. You may find that even if your firm has the raw materials to generate great ideas and client opportunities, you have to actively bring people together and insist people focus their activity. It is also important for leaders to stress to their colleagues that positioning is not just about technical capabilities, but also about client service capabilities too. As we explored in the previous chapter of this handbook, client experience has become an increasingly important factor taken into consideration when clients are evaluating which firms they want to work with; it is important, therefore, to articulate aspects of client service capability when describing why clients should choose to work with your firm.

## Sales pipeline: prospecting

Having a client-focused positioning and a deep understanding of the issues keeping clients occupied, gives a firm the best possible head start for prospecting. Prospecting is about collaborating with clients to identify and co-create solutions relevant for their specific business challenges. The difference between positioning and prospecting is that positioning is about fostering a one-to-many relationship (ie explaining a firm's capabilities to the wider market), whereas prospecting is a one-to-one relationship (ie identifying how a firm's capabilities can address a particular client's challenge). Professionals are often able to bypass the need to engage in a competitive tendering process by engaging clients in this exploratory way to design a solution to their problem.

When prospecting, leaders need to encourage people in their firm not to jump to conclusions too quickly. Challenge people to step back and look at the big picture, see the long-term opportunity and not focus on simply securing a quick deal. This requires a consultative selling approach to guide prospective clients towards a solution that works for them and can be delivered profitably by the firm. Successful prospecting conversations, therefore, will demonstrate many of the following behaviours:

- asking open and searching questions of the client to try to understand their real needs, and their business, personal and strategic drivers;

- putting to one side any preconceptions about the right client outcome or approach without first listening to the client;

- being patient and holding back on jumping to a final solution before investigating all possible options with the client;

- identifying the root cause of the client's problem or issue;

- helping the client to accept that an immediate solution – addressing the symptom not the root cause – will not necessarily be the best long-term solution; and

- challenging the client to define a precise scope and objectives for any commissioned project.

## Sales pipeline: pursuing

As the word implies, a pursuit is about actively chasing a potential opportunity, rather than working collaboratively with a client to identify a need and co-create a solution. If a client comes to you directly with an opportunity it is likely that they will have attempted to identify and shape the desired response to the need within their own organization first. In this situation professionals need to determine whether the client has shaped the brief in a way that meets their needs accurately (and so run with the scope as the client has defined it) or whether further work is needed to recalibrate the approach being put forward by the client to create a proposed solution that will better meet their specific needs.

Before starting to pursue any lead too aggressively, it is important for professionals to ask whether their capabilities are suited to delivering the outcome the client wants and whether it is possible to achieve that outcome profitably for the firm. Increasingly, data analytics can provide the evidence to help answer these questions. Analysing profitability data on similar past client assignments, for example, can suggest what an ideal client opportunity looks like, and what warning signs professionals should watch out for in a client brief that might indicate it will be a challenge to complete the work profitably.

If professionals aren't confident they can satisfy the client and make money, then it is not the right opportunity to pursue. In these circumstances, leadership comes to the fore: a team might have invested considerable time and money in developing the client relationship and so may be loath to let a potential opportunity go. Leaders need to have a conversation about the most sensible way forward and what is the best use of people's client-development time and energy. In our experience, saying no to a client opportunity and clearly explaining the reasons why, is not necessarily as damaging to a client relationship as professionals might initially believe; clients respect honesty, particularly if the adviser is also able to make a recommendation about somebody else who can help them address their issues. It is likely that the client will think of the firm when a more suitable opportunity arises in future.

It is vital to understand the buying dynamics in the client's organization when prospecting or pursuing leads. It is not uncommon for a seemingly positive opportunity to be undermined by a failure to really understand who is influencing or taking a decision in the client organization. As a leader, you need to ensure you and your team have a deep understanding of the decision-making process of the client organization, and the roles that different individuals (including individuals you may not yet have met) play in the buying process.

For high value, competitive opportunities a helpful place to start is by mapping out all the known relationships at the client organization. It is not uncommon for a professional to have a close and long-standing relationship with a handful of individuals, but for unknown individuals to be involved in the buying process for a specific project too. Use your relationships with friendly clients to ask them to help you fill in some of the blanks, rather than trying to second guess where the buying power lies. The purpose of doing this exercise is to uncover the people and teams who have hard or soft power over decisions that will affect the likelihood of winning any opportunity.

We have categorized six different levels of power and authority over buying decisions in Figure 6.3. These range from process managers, who will typically be close to the decision but relatively uninfluential, to the ultimate decision-maker who might be removed from the process but highly important. Not all of these roles will exist in every sales opportunity and one person or team may fulfil more than one role. For instance a procurement manager will probably play the role of process manager, but may also have a decision-making or influencing role.

When you have mapped the authority and influence of different stakeholders in the buying decisions you are then in a better position to:

**Figure 6.3**    Levels of authority for professional services buying decisions

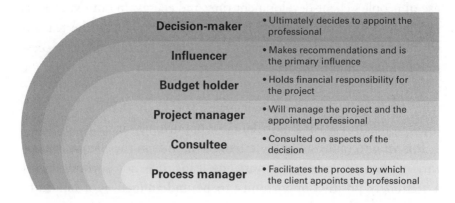

| Decision-maker | • Ultimately decides to appoint the professional |
| Influencer | • Makes recommendations and is the primary influence |
| Budget holder | • Holds financial responsibility for the project |
| Project manager | • Will manage the project and the appointed professional |
| Consultee | • Consulted on aspects of the decision |
| Process manager | • Facilitates the process by which the client appoints the professional |

- understand how well your team knows each of the key stakeholders and where there are gaps in your relationships;

- find ways of building relationships with key influencers and decision-makers who may not have been part of any discussions to date; and

- adapt your approach, emphasis and sales messages to meet the needs and concerns of those with the most decision-making power.

## Sales pipeline: proposal

If a professional has successfully followed the previous steps, the last stage of the sales pipeline should be a formality, merely a written record of the scoping conversations held so far with the client. In reality, it is often not that easy, and even the best planned opportunity can still result in a tense and time-consuming proposal stage. In our experience, although some proposals are lost in a fair fight, in most instances professional firms lose either because they were never going to be the right partner for the client for a particular piece of work, or the firm didn't do sufficient work up front to understand the client and the needs of key decision-makers ahead of submitting the formal proposal.

As a leader, there are a number of messages you should communicate to colleagues about effective proposal development that should maximize the impact of client development time. First, pay attention to price and scope: it is important that any work is priced competitively and in a way that will deliver a profit to the firm and is linked to a tight definition of scope (see Chapter 3 of this handbook for more insights on pricing and scoping). Second, think carefully about project risks: identify what factors might make a successful project outcome difficult to achieve and show the client how you intend to mitigate these risks. Third, communicate passion and enthusiasm: projects might be routine for professionals but there are often high stakes for clients, and so they want to see that professionals are committed to achieving a successful outcome and on their side from the outset.

Firms should aim to impose the same rigour on proposal management as project management; far too often firms take a very professional and deliberate approach to project management but are haphazard and badly disciplined on proposals. As a leader it is important that you remind people that project and proposal commitments need to be planned alongside each other. The latter are not subsidiary to the former.

**SUMMARY** Top tips for maximizing the strategic impact of client development initiatives

**Set expectations about how people in your firm should use their client development time**

The biggest difference leaders can make to the effectiveness of client development in their firm is to ensure that people are given clear directions about how they should focus their client development time and budgets. It is important for people to be clear not just about who they should target but also the most effective way of doing so. Although client development needs to be strategic and well-considered, encourage people to spend time out in the market and in conversation with clients and prospective clients, not stuck behind a desk spending all of their time planning. Some firms provide their professionals with minimum business development hours targets: it is important that professionals know the vast majority of this business development time should be spent with clients, rather than in internal meetings.

**Take advantage of data to make better-informed decisions about where to prioritize client development effort**

Leaders of professional firms have access to a wealth of data to help them make better-informed decisions about their firm's client development priorities. The profitability of different client segments and work types will show which opportunities and prospective clients fit the mould of high profitability/high growth potential and so which justify increased investment in time and resources. Marketing and business colleagues should be able to help you track the return on investment of specific client development initiatives; when doing so it is important to take account of the time spent planning and executing an initiative, not just the out-of-pocket outlay. Unfocused client development creates busy fools.

**Develop client relationships through proactively sharing relevant insights**

When we speak to clients of professional services firms they repeatedly say they would like professionals to come to them more often with relevant ideas and insights for their business – those that do create long-term trusted relationships and become the 'go-to' adviser when the client wants to discuss an opportunity. Clients are interested in what is happening in their market, opportunities and risks for their business they have not thought about and what peers in their sector are doing. Professionals are well placed to provide these insights but many wait to be asked rather than offer insights proactively. Many firms invest in thought leadership campaigns as a way of showcasing the kind of insight that clients are looking for, but a majority fail to coach their people how to actively share this insight with their clients and contacts as a way to build relationships. As a leader you can send a clear message to your colleagues: clients' doors are open and they are happy to take a meeting if you have relevant insights to share with them.

### Get involved in client relationship management but make sure conversations are genuine dialogues

As a leader it is important you make time for client relationship management, either by helping coordinate activity internally or by speaking regularly with the firm's clients about their experience of working with the firm. However, be mindful about the agenda when you go to see a client. Our research among CEOs shows that they want conversations to be future-looking dialogues, not just a one-sided reflection on past projects. Among the CEOs we interviewed, talking about market specific developments with their advisers was of most interest, while feedback on client service only ranked seventh in order of importance (Financial Times, Meridian West and MPF, 2012).

### Don't neglect opportunities to capture feedback at different stages of the sales pipeline

Whether they win or lose an opportunity, professionals are quick to move on, either to start work on a successful opportunity or put an unsuccessful proposal behind them. It is important to make time to find out why the result was what it was. Seek open and honest feedback from clients and as a leader you should push your teams to do this too. This can help you work out whether there are things that can be done differently when the next opportunity comes along, and what content and messages resonate most with clients and should therefore be repeated in future opportunities. Don't forget to take the time to congratulate and celebrate success internally too, particularly the efforts of team members who have worked hard to deliver high-impact client development initiatives.

# Reference

Financial Times, Meridian West and MPF (2012) Effective client-adviser relationships 2012, *Financial Times*. Available from: www.meridianwest. co.uk/wp-content/uploads/2015/02/relationshipStudy2012.pdf [accessed 04 April 2017]

# PART THREE
# **People Leadership**

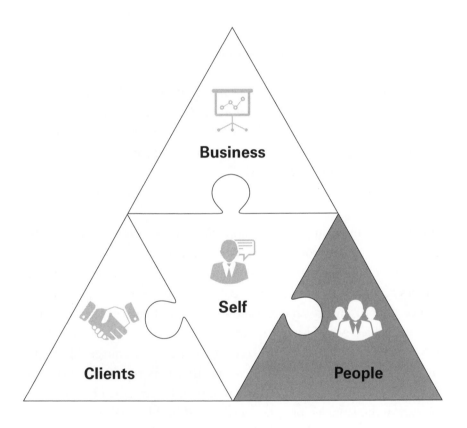

*With so much change occurring within the world of professional services, the need to connect with, and retain, your best people has become more important than ever before.*
NIGEL SPENCER, GLOBAL DIRECTOR OF LEARNING & DEVELOPMENT AT REED SMITH

*As a leader, my personal target is not necessarily my most important measure of success. The performance of the team as a whole is my priority. You have to think of professional services leadership as a team game, not an individual one.*
JOANNA WORBY, MANAGING PARTNER AT BRACHERS

*People take communication for granted, but if two thirds of my time is spent making decisions, at least a third is spent communicating them. A decision is useless unless it's been effectively communicated. Communicating with 5,000 people across 30 different countries at all sorts of different levels is a skill.*
DAVID MORLEY, FORMER SENIOR PARTNER AT ALLEN & OVERY

One of your most important responsibilities as a leader is to create and sustain an environment in which the people in your firm are empowered to perform to the best of their abilities. Successful leaders remove barriers for their colleagues to unlock higher performance and to ensure that people's focus is aligned with the firm's strategic objectives. However, getting the most out of people is not as simplistic as increasing utilization to grind out chargeable hours and hence higher profit per fee-earner; that may result in short-term financial gain but is not a sustainable people strategy. Leaders must instead make smarter people decisions to build collaborative, high-performing teams and to develop well-rounded professionals with a broad balance of skills, expertise and experiences to meet the changing demands of their clients.

As a leader, attracting, retaining and developing people is not something that you can simply delegate wholesale to colleagues heading up HR or Learning and Development functions. Successful leaders make a clear commitment to people leadership. They realize that performance management isn't a box-ticking exercise and that gathering internal feedback on strategy isn't an optional activity. The firms whose leaders understand that the skills and working practices of their people should evolve in line with clients and put plans in place to establish a continuous learning culture, have competitive advantage over the firms that don't.

Leading people within a professional services firm usually requires motivating intellectual, autonomous and entrepreneurial individuals, who typically either don't want to be led or have strong views about how the firm's leaders should best do their jobs. Failure to manage dissent and underperformance effectively can be the downfall for any leader in a partnership. Navigating the people politics of professional firms and persuading strong-willed characters to endorse and implement your strategic vision are frequently cited as challenges by people new to leadership roles.

The transition to a more strategic form of people leadership should not be underestimated. As we have noted elsewhere, leading people is different from managing them. Leadership requires an ability to build consensus, to communicate strategic decisions and to take a long-term view about professional development. This difference is recognized by Tina Williams, the chair of London law firm Fox Williams: 'Professional firms have begun to realize how important leadership is for getting the most out of their people and to build highly motivated and well-functioning teams. In my experience, many more professional firms are now prepared to devote more of their time and resources than ever before to training their people up to be successful people leaders.'

Traditionally, professional services firms had an unwritten social contract with their people: employees would work hard and remain loyal, and the firm would reward their efforts and give them a clear route to partnership. Within a generation, this social contract has broken down from both sides. The generation entering professional services today is typically less loyal to one firm, and the attractions of a portfolio career or a move to an in-house role often trump the partnership as a career aspiration. Millennials embrace change, challenge and uncertainty in a way previous generations may have shunned, and therefore expect the culture of their firm to reflect this.

From the firm's perspective, new technologies including artificial intelligence and automation tools are able to complete tasks in seconds that used to take junior professionals hours or days. Consequently, the firm of the future could be twice as profitable with half the people. The days when superior technical knowledge was enough to satisfy clients and earn a place within a firm's partnership are over. These changes mean firms cannot offer the same career stability enjoyed under the old social contract and the path to partnership is getting longer. Firms will need to find new ways to engender loyalty and manage performance.

## Key questions considered in People Leadership

The People Leadership section explores how a range of professional firms are grappling with a range of strategy, people and talent-development issues.

In *Future-fit: how to foster a commercial mindset in your firm* we consider:

- How do you link your strategic vision to the skills and personal development needs of people within your firm?

- How do you train, incentivize and inspire people to become commercially savvy professionals, not just expert technical advisers?

- How do you foster a culture of commerciality, innovation and entrepreneurship in which people are encouraged to develop new skills and competencies to meet client expectations now and in the future?

In *Motivate and collaborate: how to create high-performing teams* we explore:

- What is the best way to create high-performing teams in a professional services firm?

- What impact, if any, will the changing expectations and working preferences of millennials have on career structures and talent-management approaches in professional firms?

- How do you get colleagues to work more collaboratively to address the needs of clients?

In *Performance: how to establish a culture of continuous improvement* we consider:

- What metrics and measurements are best to track and assess the performance of people in a professional services firm?

- How can internal feedback and employee insights be used to improve performance and incentivize the right kinds of behaviours?

- How can you manage underperforming people in your firm?

# Reference

Morley, David (2014) The partnership dilemma: a special report on leadership in law in the age of disruption, *BLP and Legal Business*, October 2014. Available from www.blplaw.com/media/download/Leadership_Insight.pdf [accessed 23 March 2017]

# 'Future-fit': how to foster a commercial mindset in your firm

07

Successful leaders have a finely tuned understanding of the experiences, personal motivations and career aspirations of the people in their firm. This knowledge helps them to assess whether the skills, competencies and work behaviours exhibited by the people they lead are aligned with the firm's strategic vision. This is important not just in the context of enabling people to do a great job today, but with a view to continuing to develop the skills and competencies needed to thrive in the professional services landscape of tomorrow. The professional services leaders we interviewed all agree that fundamental changes in client expectations necessitate a similarly fundamental change in how they approach people development.

Whether you are new to a leadership role or not, it is important to build regular dialogue with the teams you lead about strengths and weaknesses, both individually and collectively. We recommend you do this often, not just as part of a structured annual review process. It is also important to pay particular attention to people leadership issues in the light of trigger events such as internal team changes (for example, new team members joining or a firm-wide restructuring) and external market changes (for example, winning new clients or targeting new markets). This process of continual reflection will ensure your teams develop the core competencies to enable them to keep pace with their changing needs. We call this becoming 'future-fit'.

This chapter focuses on how to maximize the effectiveness of your people leadership in a time of significant disruption within the professional services sector. We explore how professional services firms are innovating their approaches to skills development, and placing a commercial mindset at the forefront of their people development priorities.

# Lead by example: set the right culture in your firm

As you relax into a leadership routine, it can be easy to forget that your every action and decision is open to scrutiny by the people you lead. This is particularly true in a professional services environment with a high concentration of detail-orientated people, who can be sceptical of top-down initiatives. Yet it is not just the content of the decisions you make or the actions you take that are important, but the values and behaviours you demonstrate in following through on these decisions and actions. The values and behaviours you embody as a leader are the foundations for the culture and values of your firm. As a leader you have a uniquely powerful role to set the tone for the way in which you expect people to behave and interact with others in the firm and with clients.

Kimberly Bradshaw, managing director of HR services at accountancy firm Buzzacott, shares an example of how her behaviour sets the tone for the rest of her team:

> Because I am the team leader, everybody looks to me for team 'feeling'. That means that if I am stressed and I show that I am stressed, then the rest of the team seems to get stressed. They might even think that if I am stressed on a Monday then the remainder of the week is going to be tough. As leaders it is important to get our non-verbal message right.

The behavioural and cultural signals you send out, often unconsciously, may be more easily decoded by the rest of your team than you realize. People look to leaders for examples of appropriate behaviour to follow and to set guidelines about behaviour that won't be tolerated.

In our experience, new leaders can often get frustrated that shifting a firm's culture can be a slow process. Although culture cannot be changed overnight, it is important and helpful to begin your leadership tenure by identifying a handful of actions and changes that will send a clear message about what people can expect under the new leadership regime from day one onwards. For example, one newly appointed managing partner in a global law firm wanted to make improving the firm's internal cross-referral rate one of his leadership priorities. Within the first month of taking over he had rearranged where everybody in the office physically sat, moving them from small practice area clusters to multidisciplinary groups based on client segments. This sent a clear message that not knowing colleagues in other practice areas could not be used as an excuse for failing to explore opportunities to cross-refer work to clients.

As a leader, there are many ways to introduce small changes to your firm's culture that will have a significant impact. However, four commonly used strategies emerge from our discussions with professional services leaders:

## 1 Set expectations through your own behaviour

As a leader you should refrain from displaying poor habits or behaviours that you would not tolerate in others. Joanna Worby, managing partner of law firm Brachers, points out that the way that senior leaders behave at work sets an example for others to follow: 'Your personal profile within the firm is really important, because everybody looks to you to lead by example. I was told off recently because I sent a firm-wide email at 23.40 at night. Our HR manager kindly said to me that it didn't create a great impression, and she was right. I could have easily put it to send on delayed time. As a leader you have to take into account how your actions will be perceived by those you lead.'

Although sending a firm-wide email at midnight might not seem too problematic, it sends a signal that you expect the people in your firm to be on-call and responsive 24 hours a day. Unless the correspondence is urgent, it risks setting an unhealthy precedent that people might believe they must follow to advance their own careers.

## 2 Be as open and available for other team members as possible

Being always open and available for other team members can be difficult to achieve when there are multiple demands on your time. However, conveying a sense of accessibility does demonstrate a clear commitment to people development. Kimberly Bradshaw of Buzzacott describes how she rebalanced her diary to make more time for team members: 'I realized that in a small and very fast-growing team, people needed more of me and my time. The junior members of our team in particular needed more of the senior members of the team to be available, so we made sure there was at least one of us in the office to answer questions and provide access to that day-to-day leadership and a guiding hand. As the team leader, it doesn't matter what I am doing or have on, people still need to talk to me about something, ask me a question or to tell me something exciting.'

There is no single right way to manage this: some leaders adopt an open-door policy, some provide dedicated time in their diary for catching up with team members, and some make a commitment to walk through the office or physically sit with different team members every day or so. More guidance on managing your time to free up bandwidth for people leadership can be found in Chapter 12.

**3 Play to the strengths of your team's members**

People typically underperform in their role either if they feel they don't have the necessary skills and support to do the role well, or if they feel they have skills and experiences that are underused or not recognized by the firm's leaders. Successful leaders recognize the skills of their teams and play to these strengths and weaknesses accordingly when setting and implementing their strategic vision. This means having open conversations with people about their future development and how they can contribute most effectively, rather than focusing too heavily on negatives. Leaders have a role to play not only in addressing the weaknesses of underperforming team members but also in exploring how the existing strengths of team members can be refined and developed for maximum impact.

**4 Identify skills gaps where people need further support**

All members of a team cannot be expected to deliver every skill and competency to the same, consistently high level all of the time. There will be certain skills or tasks that some people will naturally struggle with. In Kimberly Bradshaw's view, the best leaders recognize these limitations: 'Sometimes people just aren't capable of learning a particular skill but that doesn't mean they cannot be an asset to the team. As a leader you need to find a different career path for them or a different way to employ the skills they can bring to the team. My view is that if you don't regularly review performance, and you don't give people clear messages about what you expect of them, then it is really very difficult to get the best performance out of them. The more you do work with the individuals, the more everyone gains.'

Kimberly goes on to describe how this process of identifying skills gaps also helps team members to understand how they can support the leaders in their firm more effectively: 'An important skill that you need as a leader is knowing who fills the gaps that you don't have. You need to know who plugs your own gaps so that you make a strong team, and to make sure you have every facet of your team's delivery covered. Within our team we did a strength scope analysis and we found that only a couple of us were really strategic. So we spent a lot of time working on developing the wider team's strategic skills and also on making sure that those with stronger strategic skills are freed up to do what they are best at doing.'

# Align your strategy with the capabilities of your firm's people

In the Business Leadership section we outlined the Bow Tie process for developing, communicating and implementing a strategic vision (see Figure 1.1). Central to the implementation phase of any strategy in a professional services firm is people: employees not only have to buy into what is required of them under the strategy, but they must also possess the requisite skills and capabilities to implement the strategy successfully. For example, if an accountancy firm's strategy is based on shifting focus away from compliance services to advisory services, its people need the right skills to be comfortable and credible operating in that space. It is vital, therefore, that there is alignment between your strategic vision and the capabilities of people in your firm and that you address any areas of misalignment which might limit your ability to implement the strategy.

Aligning people with strategy is an ongoing process but it has particular resonance for key people-related decisions such as recruitment, promotion, lateral hires and performance reviews. Ask yourself, for example, whether your recruitment strategy is designed to recruit people who fill gaps in the existing capability set of your firm or to reinforce the firm's existing capabilities. In our experience, too often people are recruited or promoted to partnership because they are perceived to be 'one of us' and not because their capabilities align with the firm's strategic vision.

A simple three step framework, outlined in Figure 7.1, can help you to align your desired strategic outcomes with the behaviours you expect of the people in your firm. It will help you to assess where you are today compared with where you need to be in the future.

**Figure 7.1**    Three steps to align strategy with people

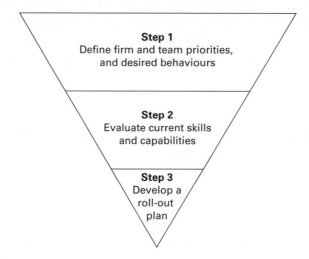

Step 1
Define firm and team priorities,
and desired behaviours

Step 2
Evaluate current skills
and capabilities

Step 3
Develop a
roll-out
plan

## *Step 1: define your firm and team priorities, and desired behaviours*

Alongside each of your strategic goals list out the capabilities and skills that will be needed to achieve these outcomes, then prioritize which will have the most impact. For each of the priority capabilities list out the behaviours and activities that you would expect people to undertake to put the capabilities into action. These should be practical things that you could describe somebody doing. For example, new client development might be high on the list of priority capabilities, but that is not a behaviour; taking new clients out for coffee to discuss their issues and challenges is a behaviour that you could imagine people in your firm doing.

Here is a worked example: achieving significant growth in China might be a core pillar of a global property consultancy's strategic plan. To achieve this goal the firm will need professionals who have experience in the Chinese market, can speak Mandarin and have relationships with Chinese buyers or investors. Other priority capabilities in this scenario might also include experience of expanding into a new market, ability to scale up a new proposition quickly and global account management. The activities that support these competencies could include creating a business case, hosting business development seminars and training up new delivery teams on the ground in China.

## Step 2: evaluate the capabilities and skills of your people

Once you have a clear idea of the competencies, behaviours and activities that will be important for the success of your business strategy, you can assess how well your firm currently performs against these priorities. This will usually be done through a mix of self-assessment, informal conversations with team members, or performance reviews and formal skills audits. Start assessing competencies at an individual level, and then cascade these up into team-wide or firm-wide competencies. For example, although a firm's employment law practice might include professionals with a high degree of strategic-thinking, the firm collectively might be underpowered for this competency. Identifying 'star performers' for a particular competency and how many of them there are, will help leaders to decide if there is sufficient critical mass to meet the demands of the strategy, or whether further investment in skills and talent is required.

A simple skills and capabilities diagnostic, like the one in Figure 7.2, can assess where gaps might exist between current competency levels and where a firm needs to be in the future. Rate skills and competencies based on where your firm is today and where it needs to be in future. Use a scale from 0 to 5, with 5 being 'strongly embedded throughout the organization' and 0 'not at all embedded throughout the organization'. Not every skill or competency needs to be rated a five out of five in the future; it is important that as a leader you develop a sense of where your firm needs to excel and where being good enough is sufficient to deliver on your strategy.

**Figure 7.2** A skills and capabilities diagnostic

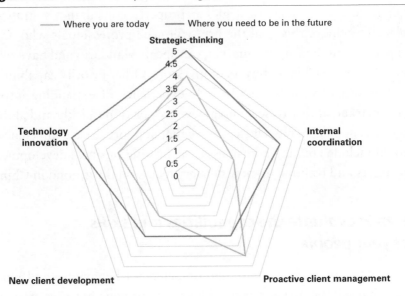

A skills audit process can be a helpful tool in itself for reinforcing a firm's strategic vision. For Tina Williams of Fox Williams, effective leaders communicate to people regularly about how they can contribute to strategy:

> One of my first lessons on developing our firm's strategy was the need to communicate regularly to the firm. You always have to reinforce in people's minds that their knowledge, skills and experience have a role to play in any strategy plan. You need to help them recognize their place within the strategy. I have found that lawyers are less reluctant to accept things if you can intellectualize it for them. Because most people find change uncomfortable, if you start by articulating how individuals need to change you typically meet with immediate resistance, whereas if you do it from the viewpoint of the shared vision for the firm and what that means for how people in the firm need to behave, then you are much more likely to get buy-in and change.

## Step 3: develop and roll out a plan for addressing skills gaps

Following steps one and two you should have a clearer idea about any skills gaps that will limit your firm's ability to implement its strategy successfully. Use this insight to create a plan to address any skills deficits. Ask yourself: which individuals or teams need most support?

What skills and competencies should we focus on? To achieve full alignment at all levels of the firm, your firm-wide skills development plan should be cascaded down to teams and individuals, thus creating a link between personal development plans and the firm's strategic priorities.

Kimberly Bradshaw describes how this process works at Buzzacott:

> Our business plan has a small number of key objectives with a clear and detailed approach for each one. There are specific activities that need to be achieved but we have kept it as simple as possible. We have linked everybody's performance objectives in the team to our business plan so they can see how their effort helps to achieve the strategic objectives. Everybody has weekly or fortnightly catch-ups with their line managers and a monthly catch-up with me as team leader to discuss their progress against these objectives, as well as formal twice-yearly appraisals. We use these discussions to identify where they are really flying, where they need additional support and, of course, their career goals.

# The commerciality deficit in professional services

Among the thousands of interviews we have conducted with clients of professional firms – with CFOs, in-house legal counsel, real estate directors, private clients and others – one common capability gap emerges time and again. Clients of professional services firms frequently identify a need for their advisers to take a more commercially savvy outlook when providing advice. They want not just technically correct solutions but also advisers who can contextualize advice in line with their commercial situation.

Examples of commercial behaviours frequently cited by clients of professional services firms as highly valued but typically lacking in their advisers include:

- keeping in regular contact and finding opportunities to meet clients at their premises;
- getting up to speed on norms, issues and trends in a given business sector;

- proactively offering a view on relevant issues and risks coming over the horizon;
- sharing insights on how industry sector peers grapple with similar challenges; and
- considering the reputational, operational and strategic implications of the advice delivered.

As outlined in the Client Leadership section, truly client-focused firms understand the wider strategic, personal and business needs of their clients and equip their people with the necessary skills and experiences to deliver commercially minded solutions. Commercially savvy professionals create greater impact by applying their technical competencies in the context of their clients' holistic needs.

Christina Blacklaws, chief operating officer at law firm Cripps, explains what commerciality means within her firm:

> We need to get our young professionals to a position where they can have a helicopter view of what is going on in their clients' businesses and the wider business environment. There is also much psychology in this: the sophisticated professionals, who will be future leaders, have a deep understanding of how people think and aspects of their behavioural psychology.

Advisers who excel at this commercial approach are sometimes referred to as being 'T-Shaped' because they have both broad business and deep technical knowledge. As a leader you need to be aware that the technical skills of people in your firm are becoming increasingly commoditized thanks to technology, smarter precedents, artificial intelligence and lower-cost competitors. Fostering a commercial mindset is one way to secure trusted, long-term relationships with clients. Firms that have taken action to address the commerciality deficit have achieved meaningful differentiation in the way that their people work with clients compared with their competitors.

While technical advice comes naturally to professionals, their commercial competencies are not always so finely tuned, not least because many professionals have never received formal training or coaching to develop commercial skills. Your role as a leader, therefore, is to encourage and challenge your teams to develop these skills and to show that your firm values a balanced portfolio of skills, not just technical expertise. You need to make the business case for focusing on commerciality. It improves the client experience by delivering better outcomes for clients, which strengthens client loyalty and improves recommendation rates. This in turn can result in more opportunities for high-margin, intellectually challenging work over the long term.

**CASE STUDY** Commercial skills development at Coffin Mew

Coffin Mew, a medium-sized, ambitious law firm based on the South Coast of England, wanted to differentiate its service by delivering commercially savvy advice to its clients on a more consistent basis. By rolling out a programme designed to foster commercial competencies the firm has benefited from real, measurable improvements in financial performance and client feedback scores. 'We are using commerciality as one of our unique selling points,' explains Miles Brown, CEO at Coffin Mew. 'We have no intentions of being one of the UK's largest law firms, but we are not a niche player. We strongly believe that true commerciality, matched with a detailed understanding of our clients' business, and embedded into the DNA of our firm, will give Coffin Mew an edge in a crowded market.'

The firm's clients include large corporates, entrepreneurs, owner-managed businesses, banks and investors, as well as wealthy individuals and families. The desire for a more commercially savvy approach was felt across each of these client segments. 'Clients love working with us and rely upon the support we give them. But our client feedback suggested that we were struggling to get the message across about the value we bring, and that is an important part of our offer,' says Miles. 'Clients told us we could do better and we listened.'

What did clients really want from Coffin Mew? 'Our clients told us they want us to understand their business better and to give advice that is commercially rooted in their business,' says Miles. 'I don't think lawyers are naturally the most commercially minded people, but we felt we couldn't ignore the message emerging consistently from our clients.'

As a result, Coffin Mew mandated that all its staff, from trainees through to senior management, participate in workshops to address their commercial skills-gap and generate action plans for improvement. 'Our staff have been coached on scoping, service delivery and pricing techniques and how to understand clients' business objectives better,' explains Miles. As part of the programme, all staff were split into teams, with partners mixing with junior lawyers, trainees and support staff to understand how to deliver coordinated commercial advice. 'We thought hard about the strengths and weaknesses of the firm, using our recent client feedback to trigger ideas,' he says.

The role of Miles and other leaders within the firm has been to encourage behavioural and cultural change and to ensure good practices are replicated. One mechanism for achieving this is the use of firm-wide, personal action plans to keep commerciality centre-stage. Another strategy the management has taken is to coordinate with HR experts in the firm. 'We are working closely with HR to implement commerciality into the competency framework, so all fee-earners are judged on it,' Miles explains.

The benefits for Coffin Mew have been significant. 'In our pitch documents we now talk about our commercial focus, saying "this is how we do it" and "this is what it means". We use commerciality as a guiding principle,' says Miles. Coffin Mew have won more work by taking this approach. 'We recently won our biggest ever client,' acknowledges Miles. 'The General Counsel we pitched to thought our proposal, which demonstrates our commercial approach, was the best he had ever read.'

Miles believes the deliberate focus on commerciality has also helped promote Coffin Mew's reputation among other professional firms: 'When we have gone out to referrers, such as accountants, banks and independent financial advisers, they have been really impressed. They are all facing the same issues that we are and are keen to find out how we have addressed commerciality in our firm.'

# Seven habits: a framework for establishing commercial behaviours

Commerciality is important to all professionals, not just the most senior, experienced partners in a firm. As Nigel Spencer, global director of learning and development at law firm Reed Smith, acknowledges, commerciality is a mindset and one that professionals should start to develop from the outset of their career:

> I want our people to be curious and really interested in the client, their business and their industries. This commercial mindset will help our lawyers to formulate their thinking about how best to use their professional knowledge to help clients. The question I want all our people to ask is 'How can I help my client succeed in their own business?' and not simply to focus on the narrow legal problem at hand.

To help people in your firm to understand how to have more commercial impact in their role we have distilled the behaviours of a commercial adviser into seven habits, as shown in Figure 7.3. The first four habits focus on applying insights about client needs, preferences and outcomes; the last three habits focus on how professionals deliver their advice to provide a better outcome for clients. How these habits manifest themselves and the relative importance of each habit, will vary depending on the type of service being delivered and a client's particular context.

**Figure 7.3**   Seven habits of a commercial adviser

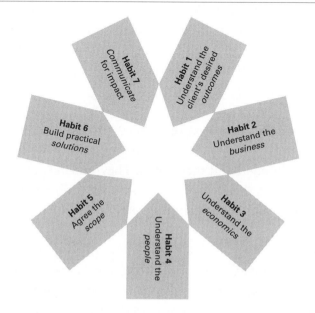

## Habit 1

**Understand the client's desired outcomes.** Commercial professionals don't launch into action following instruction from a client. Instead, they spend a proportionate amount of time up front talking to the client about their desired outcomes. For example, in an M&A deal a commercial adviser would find out what is most important for the client: achieving long-term revenue synergies, finding short-term cost savings or simply getting the deal over the line within a set timeframe.

## Habit 2

**Understand the business.** Commercial professionals understand a client's business strategy, the issues that impact the client's industry sector, and can give a view on trends likely to impact the client in the future. They use this insight to get up-to-speed with the specifics of a client's problem more quickly, and to better contextualize their advice.

### Habit 3

**Understand the economics.** Commercial professionals can do more than just read a P&L. Increasingly, there is a need for all types of advisers – from lawyers to real estate advisers and executive search professionals – to understand the financial implications of the advice they give. It is also important to be able to evaluate a client's issues both in terms of quantum and probability.

### Habit 4

**Understand the people.** Commercial professionals are sensitive to the people politics in a client's organisation without becoming political or underhand themselves. They understand the personal motivations of their client, not just their business interests, and take steps to eliminate heightened emotion from any project.

### Habit 5

**Agree the scope.** Commercial professionals spend time with the client discussing, defining and documenting an agreed project strategy. Typically this is a plan of work that sets out tasks, resources, and timelines, the role of different parties, and potential risks that could be encountered along the way.

### Habit 6

**Build practical solutions.** Commercial professionals recognize that the world in which businesses operate is increasingly collaborative, interactive, and iterative. Clients of professional firms expect their advisers to act in a way that mirrors this by collaborating to discuss options and then guiding them towards solutions, rather than always dictating the way forward.

### Habit 7

**Communicate for impact.** Commercial professionals adapt their communication style to match their client. Over the last couple of decades business communication has become more visual, more succinct and less formal. Commercial professionals use colour-coding, traffic lights and one-page summaries; they simplify their language to get a point across without talking down to the client.

# Practical ways to improve commercial impact

In our experience professionals learn best when skills development is practical and related to their on-the-job experiences. Nigel Spencer of Reed Smith agrees:

> The most effective way of boosting the skills of professional advisers is to make their learning as experiential as possible. Professionals need to be given as much opportunity as possible to apply the skills they are learning to real situations, so that they take away specific actions and begin to apply the lessons outside the learning environment.

Training that focuses on abstract concepts rather than practical examples, and requires people to make no clear commitment to change, is unlikely to have a lasting impact. Using case studies and live client opportunities or projects as examples in formal training promotes agile thinking and can help professionals to visualize more easily the benefits gained by putting their new skills into practice.

Leaders at the vanguard of people development promote a blended learning approach. The optimum blend of learning is sometimes referred to as the 70:20:10 approach, which describes the approximate ratio of experiential learning, social learning and formal learning, as illustrated in Figure 7.4. In this model formal learning interventions such as e-learning and training courses are supported with mentoring, peer-to-peer insight sharing and opportunities to develop and practise new skills through placements and increased responsibilities.

Law firm Reed Smith offers opportunities for experiential learning through a programme called CareeRS, which is aimed at fostering business skills among junior lawyers. The programme contains a mix of learning interventions ranging from a mini-MBA delivered in-house to a business masters programme co-delivered with

**Figure 7.4**  The 70:20:10 approach to blended learning

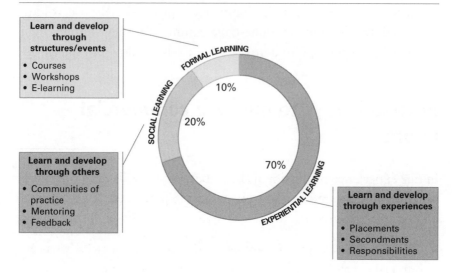

external universities. As well as developing knowledge and skills, the programme aims to help the firm's junior lawyers to build their networks within industry sectors. The firm's global director of learning and development, Nigel Spencer, describes how it has shifted people towards a more commercial mindset:

> Before beginning the programme a questionnaire indicated that some of our graduates associated the core skill set of a City lawyer with technical legal expertise. Following the introduction of the programme this was reframed into a much more balanced appreciation that understanding business finance, strategy, governance, risk versus reward and focusing on a client's commercial needs are key competencies for lawyers to succeed in their role.

Before she moved to law firm Cripps, Christina Blacklaws was head of policy at the Co-Operative Legal Services. In that role she focused on accelerating the career development of people in the in-house legal function – both lawyers and business services support – by focusing on their commercial skills:

> One of the things we did was to build a learning academy in conjunction with Manchester Metropolitan University to accommodate very flexible, but comprehensive, career paths for everybody in the business. It was important for us to build proper skills-based career paths which enabled us to be much more proactive in how we nurtured that talent.

One of the critical learnings was to identify the right people to put through programmes like this. Identifying future leaders is something that all firms need to start to do at a much earlier stage, or they risk losing their best talent to competitors.

Professional firms can also learn lessons from management consultancies, many of which place a significant emphasis on providing accreditation and recognition for people who spend time developing commercial skills. Accenture, for example, hosts a learning programme for its employees called Accenture Connected Learning, which enables employees to take online courses and access information to build accredited sector expertise. Accenture's online platform consists of more than 30,000 online courses and 25 industry-specific programmes. Employees can access a digital learning board via Accenture's mobile app that includes curated content such as videos, blogs, digital books and self-study training courses (Accenture, 2016).

As a professional services leader you play a crucial role in encouraging people to finesse their skills and behaviours to drive successful, commercial outcomes for clients and to create a culture that values continued learning and development. However, not all development opportunities have to involve investment intensive, firm-wide initiatives. There are many examples of quick wins you can implement, including:

- Post-matter video 'selfies' – recording and sharing 30-second videos on a smartphone or tablet following every client engagement is a cost-effective and time-efficient way to disseminate good practice and create a virtuous learning loop.

- Individual learning and development budgets – empower people to take control of their own learning and develop priorities by decentralizing some learning and development budgets. This limits the proliferation of 'one size fits all' approaches that are seldom effective apart from for-compliance training such as anti-money laundering. Empowering people to influence how the resource is used, in consultation with their managers, will result in better commitment to change.

- Reverse mentoring – encourage senior leaders within your firm to seek out opportunities to learn from the experiences of career professionals through reverse mentoring. These relationships not only give junior professionals exposure to senior leaders to fast-track their own development but ensure that the firm's current crop of leaders keep their skills and insights fresh and relevant.

- Business secondments – when planning client secondments identify opportunities for people to work on strategic business projects for the client, not just within in-house legal or finance departments. Even just a few days in a client's business, understanding how it operates, can bring a fresh perspective on how legal or accountancy advice is implemented once it is received by the client.

---

**SUMMARY** Top tips for developing the skills of the people in your firm

### Lead by example to set appropriate expectations

One of the most powerful tools at your disposal as a leader is your own behaviour. Think about your actions – not just what you do, but also how you do it – and whether they set the right benchmark for somebody else to follow. As a leader you can influence your firm's cultural norms by defining the boundaries of what behaviour is acceptable and what is not. Identify a small number of defining actions that you can implement early on in your leadership to signal how you expect the rest of the people in your firm to interact with their colleagues and clients.

### Identify the skills gaps necessary to implement your strategy

Don't assume that just because your firm's strategy is clearly explained everybody in the firm will be capable of implementing it from day one. You need to define what competencies and behaviours are important for success, and identify any skills deficits that need addressing. Once you have mapped out the gaps you can decide what kind of skills-development interventions will equip people with the skills they need as quickly as possible.

### Cascade firm-wide skills priorities into team and individual development plans

As a leader it is important to achieve alignment between your firm-wide strategy and how the individuals in your firm think about their own skills development. Firm-wide priorities should be communicated clearly so that everybody understands their role in taking forwards the firm's strategy and the skills they will be expected to develop to do this successfully. Firm-wide plans should be cascaded down into team plans, and team plans in turn into individual plans, so that everybody moves in the direction that will achieve strategic goals.

### Challenge your colleagues to become more commercially savvy professionals

As a leader you need to champion the many benefits of taking a more commercially savvy approach to delivering client work. What commerciality means in practice may differ by practice area or client type, but people in your firm need guidance on what they should aim towards and minimum standards to measure themselves against. This means articulating what you expect people to do more, do differently or do less to bring about more commercially savvy outcomes for clients.

### Make skills development relevant and fun for people, not a chore

It is important that people understand that skills such as commerciality are not an adjunct to their day-to-day way of working, but that these skills will enhance the impact of their existing professional skills. For this reason skills-development approaches need to be relevant to how people work in practice, not delivered in the abstract. Prioritize opportunities for experiential learning, using video, interactive technologies and role play to create learning experiences that are fun, quick and on-demand.

# Reference

Accenture (2016) Accenture invests more than US $840 million in employee learning and professional development, Accenture, 13 January. Available from: newsroom.accenture.com/news/accenture-invests-more-than-us-840-million-in-employee-learning-and-professional-development.htm [accessed 23 March 2017]

# Motivate and collaborate: how to create high-performing teams

08

One leader who has put people strategy at the top of his agenda is James Partridge, senior partner of law firm Thomson, Snell & Passmore. When he took over the role in 2008 his first priority was to address the strategic people-leadership challenges facing the firm:

> The biggest issue we faced when I took over as senior partner was our people strategy: we wanted to become an employer of choice and we needed to ensure all our people were delivering at the top of their abilities as the economy headed into recession. The first thing I did was to ensure we had the right people in the firm, because I knew that, if I had the right people on board, then they would take the firm to the right place and we would be well-prepared to weather the downturn. I spent time trying to understand what everybody was up to, how they were spending their time and where we needed to address skills gaps that were holding us back from more effectively implementing our strategy. My experience over the last decade has convinced me that my decision to focus on the firm's people from the outset was the correct one.

As James Partridge illustrates, without engaged, committed and high-performing people it is very difficult for a firm to achieve its desired business and client outcomes. Clients quickly recognize when the professionals they engage with perform below expectations and, if the client experience suffers over a sustained period, clients may look elsewhere for a better service. As a leader of a professional services firm your core asset is your people and if they are not performing as well as they should, this can have a direct, measurable impact on profitability.

One of the critical roles for any professional services leader, therefore, is to motivate colleagues to deliver high performance by giving them the right balance of clarity, confidence and autonomy. However, leaders also need to recognize that much of the latent value in their firm can be unlocked only through effective collaboration, not through excellence in niches. The complex nature of client problems often requires joined-up expertise to reach an optimum solution and this means professionals have to collaborate to deliver superior outcomes for clients. This chapter focuses on how leaders in professional firms can create high-performing teams and how they can spur effective collaboration among professionals.

# The attributes of high-performing teams

Professional firms comprise many different types of team: practice area teams, industry sector teams, multidisciplinary issues-led teams, business services teams and management and leadership teams. Whatever the nature of the team, it is important that it performs well to deliver a collective outcome greater than the sum of its individual members.

Although many people instinctively know if a team dynamic is not working as effectively as it should, it can be harder to pinpoint the practical reasons why a team underperforms. In our experience there are seven attributes which all high-performing teams display and the absence of one or more of these attributes can cause dysfunction or underperformance. These seven attributes are:

- **Commitment**

  All members of the team are clear about their goals and are committed to achieving mutually beneficial outcomes. Members of the team align their personal interests with the team goal, rather than prioritizing self-interest.

- **Trust**

  All members of the team recognize, and have trust in, the expertise and capabilities of other members of the team. Although levels of trust naturally grow with familiarization over time, teams that start out from a position of active distrust can find it difficult to surmount the lack of trust to work effectively together.

- **Culture**

  All members of the team can identify shared approaches, methodologies and common working practices that make the team efficient and effective. For example, in a high-performing team all team members may have a 15-minute catch-up meeting on a Monday to run through the week's priorities.

- **Responsibilities**

  All members of the team are clear about their own roles and responsibilities and those of others in the team. Each team member understands how his or her individual contribution helps to move the team towards its shared goal.

- **Decision-making**

  All team members perceive the way decisions are made to be fair, open and honest. Although the team tolerates, and may even encourage, different points of view, when a collective decision has been made all team members agree to implement the decision.

- **Communication**

  There is a clear flow of information between all members of the team, and regular formal and informal dialogue about progress, decisions and shared challenges. Team members communicate with each other proactively, rather than waiting for the leader to facilitate conversation.

- **Coordination**

  There are smooth transitions when actions and responsibilities are passed between team members and project management processes support a joined-up approach. In our experience one of the major bugbears cited by clients of professional firms is that information falls through the gaps when team members pass responsibility for work between each other.

To illustrate the difference between a high-performing team and a dysfunctional one, think about the following scenario. Your client, a major global soft drinks manufacturer headquartered in the UK, is seeking to buy the largest bottling plant in South America to achieve a more integrated supply chain in the region. This will reduce production costs and thus enable your client to price more competitively and grow its market share. Your client needs legal advice to get the deal done, which will involve professionals in your firm from both the UK and several South America countries, as well as a range of legal expertise including corporate transactions, property, employment, tax and pensions.

How would a high-performing team approach this scenario differently from a dysfunctional team? The following questions should help you to tease out some of the differences:

- Where are the areas where your firm might come unstuck in this scenario? What steps would a high-performing team put in place to mitigate these risks?

- How would it feel to be the client in this scenario working with a high-performing team and a dysfunctional team?

- Why would a high-performing team be likely to be make a bigger profit margin on the deal than a dysfunctional team?

- What would it feel like to be a member of a dysfunctional team trying to meet the client's expectations in this scenario?

Often it is small actions and behaviours that separate teams that perform well and those that do not. As a leader you need to be attuned to the dynamics of your teams and be alert to possible warning signs that might cause the team to underperform. Table 8.1 outlines some of the common red flags that leaders should watch out for and the potential root causes of these issues.

**Table 8.1** Warning signs of dysfunctional teams

| Team attribute | Warning signs of dysfunctional teams | Common root causes |
|---|---|---|
| Commitment | • People spend their time on activities that don't move the team's objective forward; <br> • People don't free up sufficient time to commit to the team; or <br> • People produce low quality outputs. | • Lack of clarity over the team's objectives, roles and responsibilities; <br> • Under-resourcing or over-resourcing of team; <br> • Misalignment between team members and skills required to deliver outcomes; or <br> • Insufficient time devoted to planning and scoping. |

*(Continued)*

**Table 8.1**    *(Continued)*

| Team attribute | Warning signs of dysfunctional teams | Common root causes |
|---|---|---|
| **Trust** | • People like to hold on to high volumes of work rather than delegating to others;<br>• People openly talk in a negative way about other members of the team; or<br>• People only communicate through the team leader rather than going directly to other members of the team. | • Lack of clarity over roles and responsibilities of individuals within the team;<br>• Lack of awareness of skills, experience and capabilities of other members of the team;<br>• Insufficient time spent getting to know members of the team outside a project context;<br>• Poor delegation of responsibilities from team leader to other members of the team; or<br>• Lack of regular meetings or opportunities for team to share ideas and update each other. |
| **Culture** | • There are clashes in approach, or mismatched expectations about working methods;<br>• Documents go through multiple iterations before being ready to send to a client; or<br>• The team spends little time together as a collective unit. | • Minimum service standards and expectations are not communicated to team members;<br>• Team members are not made aware of precedents or example outputs;<br>• Lack of regular meetings or opportunities for team to share ideas and update each other; or<br>• Poor briefing of team members about what is required of them in their role. |

*(Continued)*

**Table 8.1**    *(Continued)*

| Team attribute | Warning signs of dysfunctional teams | Common root causes |
|---|---|---|
| **Responsibilities** | • Tasks are often duplicated or over-resourced;<br>• Some tasks are missed and need to be completed at the last minute; or<br>• People are unclear who needs to review work before it is sent to clients. | • Lack of clear roles and responsibilities within the team;<br>• Timetable and key mile-stones are not discussed openly between team mem-bers; or<br>• Lack of regular meetings or opportunities for team to share ideas and update each other. |
| **Decision-making** | • Decisions are routinely challenged, but not in a constructive way;<br>• Decisions are taken, but never followed-through; or<br>• People do their own thing with no regard for collective decisions. | • Decisions taken by one person behind closed doors without consulting wider team;<br>• No evidence base or reasonable justification given for decisions;<br>• Alternative options are ruled out without weighing up potential benefits; or<br>• Leaders fail to communicate consequences of not following decision. |
| **Communication** | • Instructions are not followed by team members;<br>• A team member brought into the project part-way through is unclear what they need to do; or<br>• There is no clear understanding of which actions need to be delivered when. | • Leaders fail to communicate instructions to team members clearly;<br>• Lack of regular meetings or opportunities for team to share ideas and update each other;<br>• An unstructured onboarding process for new team members; or<br>• Timetable and key milestones not discussed openly between team members. |

*(Continued)*

**Table 8.1**  (*Continued*)

| Team attribute | Warning signs of dysfunctional teams | Common root causes |
|---|---|---|
| Coordination | • Multiple teams or team members wait for each other to take the lead, thus creating a coordination vacuum;<br>• Important information falls through the gaps when tasks are handed over between teams; or<br>• There are multiple iterations of documents going back and forwards between multiple team members. | • Lack of regular formal or informal communication between team members;<br>• Lack of central point of contact or a clear project coordinator role;<br>• Team members are given insufficient briefings about what is required of them and when; or<br>• Quality control processes are unclear or insufficiently robust. |

Leading a team in any professional services organization inevitably means managing personal politics and potential conflicts. Professional firms are full of self-motivated, strong-willed and highly driven individuals. However, politics doesn't have to be disruptive. Kimberly Bradshaw, managing director of HR services at accountancy firm Buzzacott, believes that actively engaging in the politics of a firm helps leaders to understand the personal motivations of others, and hence become better leaders:

> The more senior you get, the more you have to engage actively in the politics of your firm in order to get the support you need and to get people onside. There are lots of opinions that need to be garnered before change can happen, or before big leadership decisions are endorsed and implemented. Although it can seem that leaders spend much of their time navigating and trying to smooth over personal politics, if you let tensions bubble under the surface it can slowly chip away at morale and team effectiveness.

Understanding the personal motivations of team members – how they define success, their personal and professional priorities – will give you a better grasp about how team members are likely to behave and interact with others in a given situation. For example, do people feel a personal 'ownership' or responsibility for certain clients, initiatives or work types that they will feel obliged to defend from perceived attack from other people in the firm? Laying out some ground rules, aligned to the seven attributes of high-performing teams outlined above, will give team members a clear indication about how you expect them to work together. To maintain your leadership credibility, it is crucial that you are seen to follow these ground rules yourself through your engagement with others.

## Encourage professionals to collaborate

Most professional firms are expert at what they do in single disciplines. Within the boundaries of a specialist area of expertise, outputs and outcomes are easier to control, but when professionals collaborate, the risks to a successful outcome are greater and the sense of an individual or group having total control over the outcome is weakened. A criticism we hear repeatedly from buyers of professional services is that the pockets of technical expertise within professional firms are not sufficiently joined-up: as a result clients experience inconsistent levels of service, poorly coordinated handovers and they often have to repeat the same information to different team members. Clients, typically, don't experience the 'one firm' approach promised by many firms. Our research shows that, on average, the more practice areas within a firm that a client uses, the lower their overall satisfaction score. For example, Meridian West's *Mid-Market Monitor,* an annual study of buying behaviour and preferences of mid-market buyers of accountancy, shows that average satisfaction scores drop from 7.3 out of 10 for clients using a firm for one service line, to 6.9 out of 10 for clients using a firm for more than two service lines (Meridian West 2016).

However, many of the problems facing clients in a globalized world are complex and require multidisciplinary solutions. If professional firms cannot respond to this need for improved collaboration, they will miss out on potentially high-value opportunities. Being able to combine diverse expertise credibly and effectively, through integrated propositions and collaboration projects, provides a source of competitive advantage over firms that can only provide services in silos. As a leader you have an important role to articulate and communicate the opportunities for collaboration within your strategic vision, so that people can understand the practical steps they can take to make collaboration work effectively.

The firms that do make collaboration work enjoy many benefits. Harvard Law School academic Heidi K Gardner has undertaken research into effective collaboration within professional services firms. Her research shows that firms that actively encourage collaboration across different areas of expertise benefit from higher margins, greater client loyalty and competitive advantage. By analysing billing data from global law firms, Heidi Gardner has shown that the more cross-practice projects a lawyer works on, the higher the hourly rate achieved compared with peers working on single-practice projects. For example, between 2004 and 2013 the hourly rate for single-practice projects increased by 5.5 per cent compared with an increase of 11.8 per cent for multipractice area projects (Gardner, 2015).

However, genuine collaboration is about more than occasionally referring work to other members of the firm, or being a good team player. Stuart Hopper, head of EMEA practice development and knowledge at global law firm Dentons, believes that teams who collaborate effectively are self-reflective about the way in which they work together:

> Collaborative working doesn't mean bossing people about. It doesn't mean telling people that 'this is the way we do things'. I have a seen a lot of firms who say they build collaboration by just encouraging people to work well together. That is necessary but not sufficient: teams need to spend time assessing exactly what worked well and what went badly during a given project or collaborative situation. That sort of action review, typically, was not built into the legal professional services model because of the focus on maximising billable time.

Collaboration means finding new ways of working together to deliver better solutions to clients than would be achieved separately. If a tax expert (T) and a HR specialist (H) in a firm both sell services separately to a client, the value delivered could be described as T + H. But if the two engage in genuine collaboration to deliver a combined solution for their client, the potential value delivered – both to the client and to the firm – will be greater than T + H. This enhanced value principle also applies to collaboration across geographic borders or collaboration with third parties.

If the benefits of collaboration are so obvious, why do so many professional firms struggle to get it right? In our experience, there are many reasons that professionals give for not collaborating more, some of the most common of which are outlined in Figure 8.1. These reasons generally fall into three categories: a lack of knowledge (eg not knowing what other parts of the firm do), a lack of trust (eg fearing that others in the firm will do a poor job and so jeopardize client relationships), and a lack of incentive (eg people being measured on their own P&L, not on collaboration projects).

**Figure 8.1**  Commonly cited barriers to collaboration

None of these barriers are insurmountable, but overcoming them does require a cultural shift in the way people think about collaboration. This cultural shift starts with leaders placing a higher value on collaboration and breaking the concept down into behaviours and practical activities that members of the firm can follow. In our experience, professional firms that make collaboration work effectively follow some of the core collaboration principles below:

- **Lead by example** – if you want to build a culture of collaboration you need to reflect on your own priorities and how you spend your time as a leader. Find opportunities to contribute to cross-firm projects or other teams' client work to provide an example for others to follow.

- **Build internal networks** – both virtually and, more importantly, in person: internal networks are critical for overcoming trust and understanding barriers. Experiment with a range of ways to get people from different parts of the firm to socialize and share ideas. This could include weekends away, catch-ups over coffee, and 'pot luck' lunches attended by randomly selected members of the firm. Some firms even orchestrate 'speed dating' evenings where people are paired up for a few minutes to talk about recent client projects before moving on to talk to a different person from the firm.

- **Focus on real opportunities to develop reciprocal relationships** – don't just talk about collaboration, make it happen by asking team members to identify a prospective client they would like to work with and another member of the firm who could help them win that client. Going proactively to a client in a joined-up way will maximize your chance of a successful conversation.

- **Make client relationship partners accountable** – partners who have responsibility for leading key clients should be held accountable for identifying opportunities for different teams, practice areas or geographies within the firm to work with that client. The performance review process for these partners should include metrics and goals to track their collaboration efforts and results achieved.

- **Reward the outcome of collaboration, not just collaboration activity itself** – when measuring and rewarding collaboration look at impact metrics such as increases in client satisfaction, client retention and loyalty, growth in revenue for existing client accounts and new client acquisitions. In some firms a proportion of senior leaders' bonuses are tied to the firm's collective performance, not just performance within the leaders' own P&L, which helps to encourage a 'one firm' mindset.

Technology can also help to foster collaboration, particularly for firms that are geographically dispersed. Law firm RPC, for example, has won awards for its internal knowledge-sharing platform Edge, which provides an online mechanism for the firm's fee-earners to communicate, collaborate and share information. Edge operates like a social media platform for the rapid sharing of information and ideas with the firm's sector groups, and fee-earners of all levels are encouraged to use the tool to communicate with colleagues in different RPC offices. The platform also integrates with RPC's CRM (client relationship management) system to allow fee-earners to link relevant sector insights to the firm's key clients.

# Motivate millennials: the new generation of professionals

Many disruptive factors – from technology to offshoring – have fundamentally changed the resourcing model for professional firms in recent years, as well as how they develop the skills and capabilities of their people. However, one of the most disruptive forces may actually come from within firms themselves: a new generation of professionals, so-called 'millennials' or 'Gen Y professionals', who were born between the early 1980s and the late 1990s.

Joanna Worby, managing partner of law firm Brachers, describes the change she has witnessed among a new generation of lawyers entering the profession today:

> I am beginning to notice a generational change in the profession with Gen Y lawyers coming up through the firm. They need more autonomy, more communication, need to be challenged in different ways and they need lots and lots of feedback. A lot of it is about lifestyle balance, not necessarily aspiring to be a partner, and certainly not an owner. They see a law firm as a risky business, in a way that people just didn't in the past. They challenge everything now and they demand a lot more mentoring support. This requires a totally different way of managing and leading.

This generation of professionals has different expectations and aspirations for their careers. Research carried out by law firm Eversheds among lawyers aged under 35 across the globe found that 40 per cent believe the partnership model is rigid and outdated, and only 42 per cent say their current organization empowers them to reach their own potential. This generation appears frustrated that professional firms don't offer sufficient opportunities to pursue a more agile and varied career. As a result many young professionals are turning their back on partnership; only 68 per cent of the young lawyers polled by Eversheds say they plan to work in a law firm for the rest of their professional career. Instead they see in-house roles, alternative legal service providers, or portfolio careers as better suited to the autonomy, flexibility and accelerated career progression they are seeking (Eversheds, 2014).

Interestingly, the same study also revealed a strong correlation between the amount of client contact enjoyed by young lawyers and their job satisfaction. Six in ten of those polled say they meet directly with clients less than five times a month, or not at all. A similar picture emerges in the accountancy sector, where a report from global accountancy body ACCA and HR consulting firm Mercer, based on interviews with over 3,000 Gen Y finance professionals, shows that career development is one of the most motivating factors for this generation. When considering which firm to work with, millennials prioritize personal development opportunities (95 per cent cite this as an important factor) ahead of remuneration package (87 per cent), and work–life balance (81 per cent) (ACCA and Mercer, 2010).

Although this generation is attracted by high-profile, responsible and dynamic employer brands, they are not beholden to spend their entire career with one firm. A wider purpose within their professional life is also important, which is why leaders of firms should consider purpose when developing their strategic vision. Grant Thornton, a top six accountancy firm, has taken steps to respond to the increasing focus on purpose; as part of its 2020 strategy the firm has moved from a traditional partnership structure to a shared enterprise model (often referred to as the 'John Lewis' model), which means that a proportion of the firm's profits are distributed to all employees. The drive behind this move was the appointment of a new leader, Sacha Romanovitch, who was made CEO in 2015. She has stated that 'shared enterprise will allow Grant Thornton to access the ideas of all our people, who will take collective responsibility for generating increased growth and share in the reward that it creates' (Grant

Thornton, 2015). But this new model isn't just about profit distribution; central to Grant Thornton's strategy is continued investment in skills and talent by launching a skills academy and business school to support the ongoing development of the firm's people.

The historic social contract between firm and employee is being radically reshaped. Technology has a major impact on this change, with many of the tasks traditionally done by trainees or early career professionals now fully automated. Tina Williams of Fox Williams worries that young professionals may lose out on valuable learning experiences:

> People who manage to secure a training contract these days are very high calibre people. I have found they will not tolerate not being stimulated, interested and busy. They want to acquire new skills all the time and therefore they put pressure on the partners to give them access to those new experiences. However, that does mean that law firms will have to find ways of completing the lower-value tasks that have to be done. Technology and paralegals are clearly two ways of doing that. What concerns me though is that there are certain boring tasks that every trainee needs to do in order for them to understand how things work. My fear would be that this new generation is too obsessive about what skills they want to acquire without actually valuing what those lower-value tasks teach them.

It is undoubtedly true that the professions have always attracted over-achievers, who might be sensitive to criticism. However, keeping a new generation motivated and loyal requires new leadership approaches. As a leader you can set the vision for the kinds of people you want to recruit and how you wish to develop their skills and careers when they are in the firm. Given the motivational challenges presented by Gen Y professionals, it is important to recruit for attitude, intellectual curiosity and aptitude, not merely for skills and knowledge. When people are in the firm they should be provided with ongoing skills development and opportunities to put these skills into practice through business development and internal projects as well as fee-earning work. Importantly, recognize success: if people are excelling at the challenges set them, they need to know this will enhance their career progression and that they won't be held back by any perceived inflexibility in the partnership model.

# Work effectively with business services

Institutions, such as schools, hospitals and universities, rely on professional managers to share the leadership burden and to allow other staff to concentrate as much of their time and effort as possible on front line delivery. The professionalization of management within professional services firms over the last three decades has brought about the preponderance of business services roles covering areas such as HR, IT and finance. Leaders within these functional areas typically take on the day-to-day responsibility of managing the firm, its policies and processes, within their area of expertise. They create the infrastructure and systems through which fee-earners can maximize their impact on client delivery.

To get the most out of business services teams, it is important to view them not as cost centres but as pockets of expertise that help to implement the firm's strategic vision. IT infrastructure projects or marketing campaigns, for example, may require significant investment, but if they are scoped correctly and aligned with strategy, then they should generate a significant return for the firm either through increased revenue or by enhancing efficiency.

Anna Gregory started her career as a lawyer, rising to become a partner and responsible for managing the employment law practice at Farrer & Co. She now heads up the Knowledge, Learning and Development team within the same firm. In her view, professionals sometimes fail to grasp that they are not the only ones who can have a direct impact on client experience:

> It is vital not to forget the business services side. I have seen first-hand
> that a great secretary, for example, can play a massive part in winning
> and retaining clients. A highly capable paralegal is a massively more
> cost-effective resource than an expensive fee-earner. Delivering excellent
> client service involves the whole firm and to neglect the development
> and the contribution of non-fee-earning staff is a complete own goal.

Equally, leaders need to recognize when to delegate and when to seek ideas from business services specialists. Tina Williams learnt this lesson during her time as senior partner of law firm Fox Williams:

> I think it is important to have a good support group and to delegate
> whatever is possible to be delegated to those best placed to implement.

That is, of course, easier said than done because most professionals really enjoy what they do, so letting go of things can be an emotional wrench. But if you are a leader you don't have a choice. Our heads of operational functions have been increasingly involved in management decisions, which I think is a very good development. These days business services functions increasingly inform everything we do – whether that be HR, IT, finance or marketing – so I think it is imperative to bring them closer into the fold.

In our experience, there are five principles successful leaders follow to maximize the contribution of business services teams within their firm:

## 1 No divisive language

Unhelpful language such as 'non-lawyers' or 'non-accountants' can create unnecessary division and cause business services staff to feel their contribution to the firm is less valued than fee-earners. Successful leaders recognize and champion the specialist knowledge and experience business services staff have in driving forward the strategy of their firm, and take others in the firm to task when they don't treat business service staff with respect.

## 2 Clear management reporting lines

In many professional firms it is now routine to find business services leaders as part of the firm's Management Board or Executive Committee. If they are not full Board members, heads of business services should be given clear reporting lines into the firm's leadership and invited to attend and present at Board meetings regularly. They should be challenged and supported by the firm's leadership but never micromanaged.

## 3 Proximity between strategy and implementation teams

Leaders should consult business services on important strategic decisions to ensure alignment between strategic decisions and their implementation and to enjoy the benefit of the wisdom and experience of business services professionals. In many firms it is not uncommon to find implementation teams too far removed from those making strategic decisions, which can lead to conflict, lack of trust or ineffective implementation.

**4 Cross-functional collaboration**

Increasingly, many strategic projects require collaboration between different business services departments. It is important, therefore, that, in addition to any Board-level discussions, business services leaders have a mechanism by which they can get together regularly to share priorities and discuss opportunities to work together to deliver on the firm's strategic vision.

**5 Opportunities for internal secondments**

Some firms have begun to offer secondments for fee-earning staff into business services departments, either as part of their early career training programme or their transition towards leadership roles. These secondments not only help to develop a greater understanding of the role of business services but also build skills in areas such as strategic thinking and project management.

---

**SUMMARY**    Top tips for unlocking higher performance in your teams

**Align personal goals and motivations with team goals**

High performance starts with people committing to a shared goal because without a shared sense of purpose it is difficult to get everybody to move in the same direction at a similar pace. Understand what motivates individual members of your team and use this insight to shape team roles and responsibilities to play to people's strengths and motivations. This is particularly important for the generation of professionals entering work today who are instinctively less loyal to one firm and will seek opportunities to challenge themselves and learn new skills.

**Recognize there are different career paths for professionals and value each of them**

The skills needed to be a successful professional are multiple and various, yet most firms still place the greatest emphasis on technical expertise. Forward-thinking firms realize that there is a benefit in accommodating people with varied skills and capabilities: deep technical specialists, generalist advisers, rainmakers and business developers, project managers and people leaders. A balanced scorecard allows you to assess somebody's contribution to the firm holistically, and to make a case for career progression based on factors other than client billings.

### Be aware of the warning signs of dysfunctional teams and act proactively to turn things around

As a leader you need to be attuned to potential warning signs of dysfunctional teams. Spot these signs early and work with team members to determine the root cause and then create an action plan for addressing the issues. In our experience, most team dysfunction in professional firms is caused by lack of communication, lack of clarity about roles and responsibilities and poorly executed handovers between team members.

### Celebrate the outcomes of collaboration, not just collaboration itself

Collaboration can be difficult but emphasize the major upsides during your conversations with others in the firm. Failing to collaborate means potentially missing opportunities for high-value, high-margin client work. Increasingly, clients favour multidisciplinary solutions and expect their advisers to provide a joined-up service when multiple teams and offices are involved. Draw attention to examples of positive collaboration and celebrate the beneficial outcomes such as growth in financial metrics or increased client satisfaction and loyalty.

### Don't undervalue the contribution your business services leaders make to strategy implementation

As a leader you need to have a high degree of self-awareness about your own capabilities and your limitations, as well as those of the people around you. Business services leaders have specialist knowledge and skills and are there to help you create and implement your strategic vision successfully. It is important to know when to draw on their expertise and experience and when to give them ownership of projects without interfering or micromanaging.

# References

ACCA and Mercer (2010) Generation Y: realising the potential. Available from: www.accaglobal.com/uk/en/technical-activities/technical-resources-search/2010/july/generationy-realising-the-potential.html [accessed 23 March 2017]

Eversheds (2014) 21st century law firm: a report exploring the views of the emerging generation of lawyers. Available from: www.eversheds-sutherland.com/global/en/what/publications/21stclawyers/index.page [accessed 23 March 2017]

Gardner, Heidi K (2015) When senior managers won't collaborate, *Harvard Business Review*, March. Available from: hbr.org/2015/03/when-senior-managers-wont-collaborate [accessed 23 March 2017]

Grant Thornton (2015) *Strategic Review 2016*. Available from: www.grantthornton.co.uk/globalassets/1.-member-firms/united-kingdom/pdf/publication/2016/strategic-review-2016.pdf [accessed 23 March 2017]

Meridian West (2016) Technology and automation: what do buyers of professional services want? 21 December. Available from: www.meridianwest.co.uk [accessed 23 March 2017]

# Performance: 09
# how to establish
# a culture of
# continuous
# improvement

Successful professional services leaders advocate and celebrate the right behaviours in their firm, but also confront the wrong behaviours through conversations with the people who aren't conforming to the expected standards of behaviour. As we outlined in the previous two chapters, leaders have a critical role to play in setting expectations and minimum standards, and to encourage people to acquire the skills and capabilities they need to deliver commercially savvy solutions for clients and to collaborate successfully with their colleagues.

However, leaders also have an important role to play in establishing a culture of continuous improvement so that performance in their firm doesn't remain static. As clients of professional firms become increasingly demanding about service experience and added-value, and their business, personal and strategic challenges become more complex and interrelated, professionals need continually to refine and enhance the way they work to keep pace with client expectations. Firms that don't embed continuous improvement into their ways of working will find themselves falling short of client expectations and being overtaken by competitors in the long term. This chapter is designed to help leaders maximize the usefulness of the continuous improvement tools at their disposal such as performance reviews and internal feedback. It also provides guidance on how to manage underperformance should anybody in a firm fail to meet agreed expectations.

# Don't just tick boxes: maximize the value of performance reviews

Most professional services firms have an established performance-review process, which will more than likely involve a periodic review of people's recent performance – key achievements, outcomes met and areas for improvement – alongside target-setting for the next period. In the majority of professional firms this process will be led by a person's direct line manager and may also involve contributions from direct reports, other members of the team or other leaders within the firm. The performance-review discussion and annual goal-setting typically incorporate related issues such as learning and development needs, remuneration, career progression and bonuses.

The pen portrait of a typical performance review outlined above is very process-orientated. It involves capturing and discussing information, form-filling and setting goals at a single point in time. For that reason, an annual appraisal can sometimes be viewed unfairly as a box-ticking exercise: at best a series of forms that have to be completed to present the evidence to justify a bonus or promotion, at worst something that gets in the way of fee-earning time or other priorities. This narrow attitude overlooks the important role that performance reviews can play in giving space and time for people to reflect on their personal development needs.

Although the majority of professional firms do treat performance reviews with the importance they deserve, the process itself can be static and unhelpful for tracking personal development in real time. Some firms (such as IBM, as illustrated in the case study opposite) are changing their performance review processes to become more agile and responsive to the way people's careers and development needs change over time. The guiding principles behind these changes is to facilitate more regular conversations about performance, to encourage ongoing learning and to collate and showcase examples of good practice which can help to improve the way people in the firm work.

**CASE STUDY**  IBM rewrites the rules on performance reviews

In February 2016 Ginni Rometty, Chairman and CEO of IT services giant IBM, announced that she had decided to scrap IBM's annual performance review cycle in favour of an app-based system called Checkpoint. This new system enables IBM employees to take greater ownership of their professional development and goal-setting, and to provide more frequent feedback on progress throughout the year (Zillman, 2016).

IBM wanted to move away from performance management being viewed internally as a static and low-value exercise. Rather than have employees set goals at the beginning of a year, only to be reviewed at a much later date, IBM's new system allows employees to set shorter-term goals. Managers are expected to commit to providing formal feedback on these goals at least once a quarter and to discuss progress with employees.

At the end of each yearly cycle IBM's employees will then be assessed on five criteria:

- business results;
- impact on client success;
- innovation;
- personal responsibility to others; and
- skills.

Like many firms at the vanguard of people leadership, IBM has recognized that the business environment is rapidly shifting and the changes it has introduced are designed to reflect more effectively how people work and how their roles and responsibilities change over the course of a year.

So, how did IBM design its new performance-management process? According to Ginni Rometty, the firm turned to its 380,000 employees in 170 countries to crowdsource the process: 'Our chief human resources officer posted a message on our internal social media platform asking employees to share their ideas for a new performance management system. The post received 75,000 views and 2,000 comments from employees.' By involving employees directly in the design of the new system, the firm believes that people will be more engaged and take stronger ownership of their own career development.

When reviewing performance and setting goals, it is important for leaders of professional services firms to link what is being measured, and also rewarded, with the behaviours and competencies that are needed to move forward the firm's strategy. Looking solely at technical expertise and billable hours neglects the contributions people make to the firm in other ways such as business development, team leadership and client experience. Although almost all firms pride themselves on, and emphasize in their marketing collateral, their commitment to client service, recent research among CMOs and heads of business development in professional firms found that only 21 per cent of firms currently reward people based on the quality of client service they deliver (Beddow, 2017). To drive the right kind of performance in their firm, leaders need to grasp the opportunity to close the gap between rhetoric and what is measured and rewarded.

To get the most from performance reviews it can be helpful to use a balanced scorecard approach, reviewing performance against a wide range of measures. This helps to ensure that people don't prioritize one set of skills and capabilities at the expense of another. A framework incorporating the four elements of the Leadership Triangle – business, clients, people and self – is a useful way to measure somebody's contribution to different areas of the firm.

In addition, it can be helpful to build evidence from a wider range of sources including client feedback and client testimonials, profitability of client assignments (not just fees billed), and collaboration or internal referral rates. Goal-setting is an important part of the process, but these goals should be realistic, achievable and aligned with strategy. Ideally, goals shouldn't be front-loaded (ie all to be achieved within a month) or end-loaded (all to be achieved just in time for the next review) but should be designed to support ongoing development, with clear development milestones throughout the year.

Feedback discussions should be open, honest and constructive, with a focus on celebrating achievements and understanding opportunities for, and barriers to, further development. As a leader you need to create space in which people feel comfortable with a balance of challenge, support and reflection. The following questions may help you to get the most out of performance review conversations:

- What achievement are you most proud of during the last six months? Why?
- What would you do differently if you were to repeat the last six months over again? Why?
- Where have you made the most significant contribution to the firm beyond fee-earning work?
- How do you feel you can help the firm to achieve its strategy over the next six months?
- What skills and competencies will you need to work on over the next six months to enhance your performance further?
- Who in the firm would you like to work more closely with over the next six months? What do you hope to achieve through this collaboration?
- What lessons from your recent experience would you pass on to other members of the firm?

# Build ongoing learning into the project-delivery process

As we explored in Chapter 7, the majority of learning that professionals undertake should be experiential and directly linked to the way in which they work with clients. With this in mind successful leaders encourage others in their firm to turn client engagements into active learning experiences to drive continuous improvement and find ways of doing things better in future. Doing so benefits the firm and its clients, because future engagements will run more efficiently (and hence more profitably) and with a greater awareness of what is most valued by clients (and hence will increase client satisfaction).

Anna Gregory of law firm Farrer & Co agrees. Early on in her own career she found experiential learning was the most effective way to improve client relationship skills:

> The knee-jerk assumption for a lot of professional firms is to treat formal training as a panacea. I know from first-hand experience that formal training sometimes misses the mark, and even good training is often forgotten about almost as soon as people walk out of the room. Really effective

training requires further reflection and ideally some sort of active follow-up to embed the learning properly. I also believe that firms should place a greater value on learning at the feet of others: I picked up great insights about how to handle client relationships that way. On-the-job learning can get neglected in the face of cost and time pressures but that is a false economy in the long run.

Building learning and continuous improvement into project processes requires setting aside sufficient time for reflection and feedback both during and at the end of client engagements. It is not uncommon for firms to request formal feedback from clients but few firms formalize the collection and analysis of internal feedback. This can be done either through a face-to-face wash-up discussion among the team or through individual feedback questionnaires for self-reflection. For example, at the end of an audit the delivery team could sit down to discuss what worked well, what could have been improved and what should be approached differently in future; these learnings can then be built directly into how the team plans and executes the next audit for the client.

The kinds of questions you might find it helpful to get people in your firm to discuss as part of their reflection are outlined below. If you already ask clients for feedback, it can be useful to mirror the criteria used by clients to assess performance when asking colleagues internally to reflect on their performance. This will allow you to spot any gaps in perspective between the client and the delivery team.

- How interesting and engaging was the work?
- How pleasant was the client team to work with?
- Did the project help to develop the team's skills and competencies? If not, why?
- How did the team perform and what were the areas for improvement?
- What approaches worked well that could be repeated for future projects?
- What mistakes were made and how could we avoid making them again if we were to do a similar project in future?
- What could the client have done to make our lives easier? How might we communicate this more effectively to other clients in future?

- How will we maintain an ongoing relationship with the client?
- What opportunities have arisen for us to introduce other colleagues to the client?

The insights gained from internal discussion can be correlated against client feedback. Client views will tell you if there are any issues from the client perspective but the internal views will help you to understand the root causes of those problems and how they could be avoided in future. For example, if a client has given lower feedback scores for responsiveness and meeting deadlines, the internal feedback may reveal that team members felt the project was under-resourced and that if they were to undertake a project of a similar scope in the future they would recommend increasing the team size as a way of not crunching up to deadlines.

Firms on the cutting edge of feedback are using the insights gained both internally from teams, and externally from clients, to support ongoing people development. Best practice case studies, videos, top tips and templates can all be shared within the firm to guide others on how best to approach similar work or client issues. By collating and sharing these insights firms can avoid one of their perennial weaknesses: reinventing ways of working and service methodologies from scratch for each new client engagement, rather than finding opportunities to standardize and replicate good practice. Making a conscious effort to take learnings from every client experience and to share these lessons within the firm, will help people to understand the benefits of continuous improvement and actioning feedback from clients and colleagues.

# Grasp the nettle: managing underperformance

Managing underperformance is one of the more difficult tasks a leader has to face. Nobody likes to bring confrontation into a consensus-driven and collegiate environment, and it can be particularly challenging to provide negative feedback to people with whom you work closely on a daily basis. However, underperformance needs to be dealt with before it is allowed to escalate. As a leader it is your responsibility to set cultural norms about the kinds of behaviour you will tolerate and what is not acceptable. If you fail to deal with underperformance early on, it could encourage others to adopt poor behaviours and lead to negative client experiences.

Anna Gregory of Farrer & Co believes that leaders need to be open and honest with their people and call out underperformance early on, rather than pretend there are no problems:

> Honesty and empathy go a long way, though in my experience the former is often lacking when dealing with individuals who might be underperforming for whatever reason. I have lost count of the number of times when, in my previous role as an employment lawyer, I advised a client on a dismissal where the individual's appraisal painted them in pretty glowing terms. In my experience there is usually a way of having difficult conversations about underperformance that leaves the individual concerned feeling supported rather than stitched up, but to get there you need to have open and straightforward conversations along the way.

When having a conversation about underperformance it is important to figure out the root cause. Is it caused by a lack of information or understanding, or a mismatch of expectations about what is required in the individual's role? Or is the root cause attitudinal, for example a lack of respect for colleagues, bullying behaviour or apathy towards client work? Clearly as a leader you need to know where to draw the line about what is underperformance that can be resolved positively and what is considered unacceptable behaviour such as bullying. Understanding the root cause will help you shape a solution that will enable the individual to improve, and to recalibrate expectations about the outcomes you would like them to achieve in future, without the need for personal confrontation.

**CASE STUDY**  Tina Williams of Fox Williams on how to deal with underperformance

Tina Williams co-founded London law firm Fox Williams in 1989. Over the last three decades Fox Williams has grown into a firm with an annual revenue of more than £20 million. Between 2005 and 2013 Tina was the firm's senior partner and in 2013 she became chair of the firm. One of the major leadership lessons Tina learnt during her time as senior partner is to deal with underperformance early. 'It can be very tempting to kick problems into the long grass and hope that they will become better of their own accord which, of course, they never do,' says Tina. 'In my experience, problems just get worse and worse if they are not dealt with in a timely manner.' One of the underlying causes of sustained poor performance can be a failure to deliver difficult messages at an early stage before the issue has become completely unresolvable.

Many leaders in professional services firms sit on problems because they are reluctant to have difficult conversations with their colleagues. Tina's view is that these conversations don't have to be confrontational to resolve issues effectively: 'One of the skills I learnt as leader is how to communicate difficult messages to others in the firm clearly. Nobody wants to be the bearer of bad tidings, so it is important that difficult messages are framed constructively so that you can get buy-in to what needs to happen to remedy a particular situation.'

During her tenure as senior partner Tina encountered instances where she had to deal with colleagues performing below the expectations set by the firm's leaders. 'Most of the issues I have faced have been around the way that people conduct themselves, not in the sense of behaving badly, but in the sense of spending their time fruitlessly,' says Tina. 'I had a discussion with one partner about how he actually spent his time and where his time might be better spent. Together we analysed his time-recording data and agreed a joint plan about where he could make improvements. We had regular meetings to track his progress and over a period of about fifteen months there was a noticeable improvement. As a result he took a more disciplined approach to the way in which he spent his time and was able to make a valuable contribution to the firm.'

What has Tina learnt from her experience about dealing with underperformance? 'I always prefer the carrot to the stick,' she says. 'However, this requires you as a leader to deal with issues quickly and to avoid having endless discussions. Don't mistake endless conversations for real action that resolves the issue at hand.'

---

**SUMMARY**  Top tips for sustaining continuous improvement

### Frame performance reviews as reflective, extended learning conversations

Encourage others in your firm to see the performance review process or appraisal system as a way of identifying opportunities for building on existing strengths and capabilities to enhance their performance. Performance reviews completed for their own sake will never be particularly fruitful. Ask reflective questions that allow you to understand people's personal motivations and how they would like to focus their own future development.

## Use a balanced scorecard approach to assess people's contribution to the firm

Conversations about performance should consider the variety of ways that people contribute to professional firms. As a leader, think about how you would expect people at different stages in their career to focus their time, and reflect this in how you balance any performance review conversations. For example, those on the track to partnership are likely to spend more of their time on business development, taking responsibility for leading client relationships and mentoring and coaching junior fee-earners. How their performance is measured and rewarded should reflect this balance of time and the behaviours you want to promote.

## Set performance goals with interim milestones

Performance goals should have interim milestones and measures that will enable you to track whether people make sufficient progress throughout the year. Make time to review performance during the year, not just at fixed intervals such as appraisal. Allowing people some ownership over their own development time and budget will help them to focus on tailoring learning and development interventions to meet the goals agreed as part of their performance review.

## Integrate internal team feedback into process improvement and project planning

Following completed client assignments encourage team leaders to hold internal wash-up sessions to review team performance and identify areas for improvement that can be built into the way in which teams work with clients in future. Integrate feedback from clients along with internal feedback to understand the root causes of client frustrations and to capture good ideas for future improvements. Don't rest on your laurels: each client engagement represents a potential learning experience for every member of your team, including yourself.

## Don't let underperformance go unchallenged

Leaders who ignore underperformance do so at their peril. Poor behaviour internally sets bad examples for others to follow, particularly if it goes unchallenged by senior leaders in the firm. If dealt with early on, people are usually more open to change the way they behave. Agree reasonable steps you would like people to take to address their performance and the support they can expect from you and others to help them improve. Keep progress regularly under review, and don't neglect saying so if performance hasn't improved at the rate you would expect.

# References

Beddow, Alastair (2017) Marketing benchmark 2017: turning client focus into competitive advantage, *PM Magazine*, January. Available from: www.pmforum.co.uk/knowledge/surveys/marketing-benchmark/marketing-benchmark-2017.aspx [accessed 23 March 2017]

Zillman, Claire (2016) IBM is blowing up its annual performance review, *Fortune*, February. Available from: fortune.com/2016/02/01/ibm-employee-performance-reviews [accessed 23 March 2017]

# PART FOUR
# Self Leadership

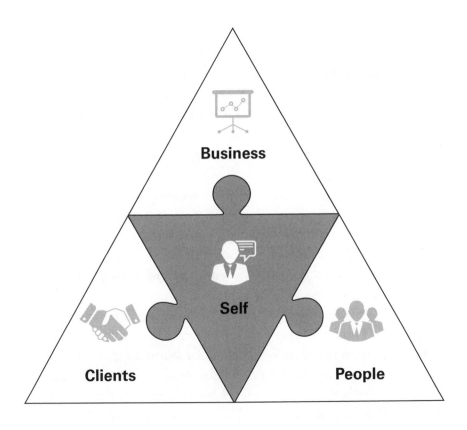

*I joined Brachers as a trainee solicitor in 1991 and I became partner in 1999. I didn't really have any leadership training as I made that transition. In 2006 I changed disciplines and that was when I became a team leader: I moved over from litigation to employment. That was really interesting because it meant I was leading a team of lawyers who had more technical knowledge within their area of expertise than I did. It made me aware of the other skills I could bring into the group: strategic thinking, commercial awareness, challenging what they do and why they do it.*

*That experience taught me how to be a good delegator because for the first time I was able to delegate to people who had more technical knowledge than me. I had confidence whereas, up to that point, I used to think that nobody could do as well as I could. To be a good leader you need to delegate, you can't take it all and do it all yourself. You do need to know where your limitations are and when you need to seek assistance. The transition to leadership can be quite grounding actually.*

*Moving to take on a leadership position was one of the most rewarding things I have ever done and to see the team thrive was amazing. I learnt so many things, such as where I can add value to support the fee-earners in my team and how to manage client relationships without doing the fee-earning work myself, which I had never done before.*

*I learnt to believe in myself that I could manage and lead other people well. I had never been on the business side of the firm before, I had only ever worked with individuals. I learnt a lot more about the structure of teams and the politics of teams and how you can develop individual strengths to work well together as a team. These are all highly valuable skills and learning experiences I have been able to draw on in my role as managing partner at the firm.*

JOANNA WORBY, MANAGING PARTNER AT BRACHERS

At the centre of the Leadership Triangle is 'self': you as a leader. The experience described by Joanna Worby – limited leadership training coupled with strong personal motivation, getting to grips with a rapid learning curve – is far from unique. Many leaders in professional services firms find themselves regularly pushed outside their comfort zone and have to learn new skills to tackle new experiences and to solve new problems successfully. This section on self leadership is designed to help you embrace, and successfully overcome, the kind of personal challenges that Joanna describes. It will help you to act in ways that maximize your leadership impact and enhance your desired outcomes for business, client and people leadership.

As the role of the professional services leader becomes more complex and the pace of change in the external environment continues to accelerate, leaders need to develop a more adaptive style. This is important both at a micro and a macro level in order to achieve optimum results for individual leadership tasks and across the portfolio of leadership needs within your firm. Just as professionals wouldn't expect to become a qualified accountant or lawyer without a significant investment in learning, training and experience, aspiring leaders shouldn't let leadership creep up on them by overlooking the need to invest in their personal development. Proactively preparing for leadership avoids the all-too-common scenario of having to back-fill the necessary learning, training and leadership experience only once you are a new leader in the spotlight.

It is very easy to find that the demands of business, client and people leadership drain the amount of time available to you for self-reflection and proper self leadership. In this section we explore strategies used by successful leaders to maintain a balance between competing demands on their time and attention, and how they challenge themselves to improve their leadership style and credibility. Being a leader isn't something that stands still: it is something that you need to constantly devote time to developing and applying.

It can be very lonely at the top. As Philip George, the former managing partner of East Anglian law firm Birkett Long, observes, the road isn't always plain-sailing for aspiring leaders:

> Don't expect to be the most popular person in the office, you certainly won't be! It goes with the territory that difficult decisions have to be taken, and it is inevitable that in taking them you will stand on some people's toes. If popularity is important to you, don't be managing partner. Respect, rather than popularity, is what you should be hoping to secure.

But the leadership rewards can be great too. Leaders who are able to inspire, motivate and empower others within their firm are most likely to have significant, long-term leadership impact. These are the leaders who will secure a prosperous future for their firm, its people and its clients, while thriving and enjoying the personal challenge of leading a firm.

## Key questions considered in Self Leadership

In the three chapters in the Self Leadership section, we will explore answers and case studies for the following questions:

In *Forward reflection: how to assess your leadership potential*, we consider:

- What are the different types of leadership and how do you compare with other leaders?

- How do you assess your leadership motivations and your potential leadership style?

- How do you prepare yourself to take on a leadership role?

In *Capability: how to develop the skills, competencies and experiences to be a successful leader*, we answer:

- What is the right mix of skills that you need to develop to be successful as a leader?

- How should these leadership skills and competencies be applied in practice?

- How do you maximize the impact of your leadership to deliver better business, client and people outcomes?

In *Balance: how to succeed as a leader without burning out*, we consider:

- Is it possible, or even desirable, to take on a leadership role and maintain your chargeable hours targets?

- How do you delegate effectively to avoid filling your time with legacy challenges?

- How do you make the best use of your diary to balance the competing demands on your time?

# Forward reflection: how to assess your leadership potential

Few people go into the professions seeking out a leadership role. The reasons why you want to be a leader aren't usually given much critical thought, particularly as many people find themselves in leadership roles either reluctantly or serendipitously, rather than as a result of a deliberately planned career trajectory. Even those people who actively aspire to leadership find that they are less than certain about their motivations when they externalize their reasons and really challenge themselves to describe what kind of leader they aspire to be.

Many of the leaders of professional services firms we have encountered say they miss being hands-on, getting stuck-in to deliver client work. Others do not see this as a problem, or have found ways of adapting to the change. Everybody is in agreement, however, that taking on a leadership role involves a different dynamic from being a technically excellent professional.

It is not uncommon, even among successful leaders, for leadership to creep up on people: they accept a promotion or a career step forward and leadership comes as a part of the package, whether it is sought out or not. It is not that people are usually shy of taking on leadership responsibilities but that the leadership role they find themselves occupying is a poor fit with their aspirations, skills and leadership style. Spending sufficient time reflecting on why you want to be a leader, and what you want to achieve through your leadership, will help you to understand, articulate and find a leadership role that is a good fit for you.

As George Bull, senior tax partner at accountancy firm RSM, acknowledges, professionals need to be clear in their own minds why they want a leadership role. In his own experience this transition to leadership requires a mindset shift to think like a 'business owner': 'For business-level leadership roles, you need to identify people who have the potential to think like business owners, who realize that they are not in the firm to be solicitors or architects or accountants, but to run a profitable business by selling legal or architectural or accounting services. That is a huge mindset shift.'

This chapter is designed to help you think through how well prepared you are to embrace the mindset shift that George Bull describes, and to describe how to map out your potential journey to a leadership position.

## Assess your potential: six leadership attributes

Leading implies that someone or something is following and that the followers have bought into the ideas and vision put forward by the leader. It is this ability to influence, create and maintain followers that differentiates people typically highlighted as successful leaders. Think about a range of successful leaders you admire from the world of sport, politics, arts or business and you will realize that leadership is a multidimensional skill, where success comes in many different forms. But they are likely to have one thing in common: a commitment to leadership and maximizing their personal impact in whatever field they have chosen to excel in.

To help define what kind of leader you aspire to be and to assess your leadership potential, we have broken leadership down into six attributes. These six attributes are set out on the 'Personal leadership dimensions map', a copy of which has been filled out in Figure 10.1. This tool shows you how the different elements of your leadership combine. It should help you to identify your leadership type today and how you might want to develop it in the future.

**Figure 10.1** Personal leadership dimensions map

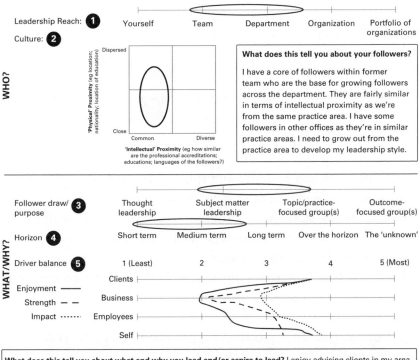

**What does this tell you about your followers?**

I have a core of followers within former team who are the base for growing followers across the department. They are fairly similar in terms of intellectual proximity as we're from the same practice area. I have some followers in other offices as they're in similar practice areas. I need to grow out from the practice area to develop my leadership style.

**What does this tell you about what and why you lead and/or aspire to lead?** I enjoy advising clients in my area of specialism. I understand the practice area's performance but struggle with linking this to the firm-level results.

| Style | Authoritative | Directive | Participative | Inspirational | Laissez-faire |
|---|---|---|---|---|---|
| # of times used | 8 | 10 | 5 | 2 | 0 |
| % of times used | 32% | 40% | 20% | 8% | 0% |
| How adaptive are you between styles? (H/M/L) | L | | | | |
| % of times you deploy the optimum style | 50% | | | | |

**What does this tell you about how you lead?** I tend to be more directive and manage people rather than trust and lead. I need to develop and deploy a wider set of styles.

**Overall what does this identify?** I have a good base of followers but need to consolidate this by developing a wider selection of leadership styles and consciously use them in different situations to try and get better performance/outcomes from the team. I also need to develop confidence outside my practice area and in the wider firm.

Each of the six attributes on the map is represented as a continuum. There is no right or wrong position to be on the continuum for each of the six attributes. In reality, where you will be on each continuum is likely to change over time – as your responsibilities change, as the external market evolves. When identifying your leadership style, think about where you feel most comfortable operating on the continuum, and where you aspire to be. Try to take an objective view and ask yourself two questions: given the leadership challenges facing my firm, which leadership position will create optimum impact? And do I have the potential to occupy that leadership position in future?

## Attribute 1: leadership reach

**Yourself – team – department – organization – portfolio of organizations**
By leadership reach we mean what, or who, you are leading. Traditionally, leadership reach was easier to map as it directly equated to your job title and role profile. However, organizational structures today can be more amorphous. You may have direct and indirect leadership positions, at multiple points on the continuum. The continuum starts with 'Yourself' because many professional services firms contain experts who lead a particular subject matter, sometimes called 'thought leaders', who have no direct followers within their firm but are acknowledged in the wider marketplace as leaders within their own niche of expertise.

## Attribute 2: culture – intellectual proximity/physical proximity

**Close common – dispersed common – close diverse – dispersed diverse**
Leaders create empathy and affinity with their followers. In many cases this affinity is as a result of the culture of the firm, its shared norms, environment and collective experiences. Culture is what binds us together to create a similarity in the way we think. In a professional services context, professional affiliation has a major impact on professionals' frames of reference. The route to becoming a professional usually involves a period of education that is driven by a professional body and which sets professional standards as well as risk appetite and how others think about different business or technical issues.

Leading a team of people with a common culture can be very different from leading a team with a diverse set of cultural views.

How proximate are you to the people you lead? We measure proximity on two axes: physical proximity and intellectual proximity. Physical proximity might include the location in which people work or live but also the location in which they were brought up or educated. This dimension is increasingly important as firms look to recruit from a more global and diverse talent pool. Figure 10.2 shows how leaders might straddle different spaces on these two axes depending on the precise nature of their leadership role.

**Figure 10.2** Examples of leadership roles and their cultural impact

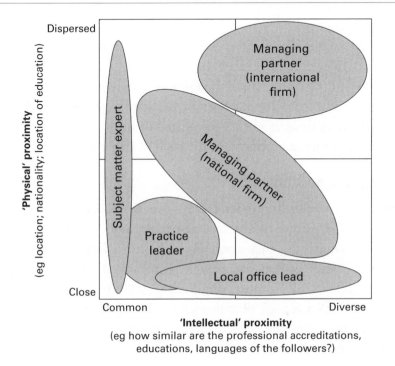

## Attribute 3: follower draw/purpose

**Thought leadership – subject matter – topic focused group(s) – outcome focused group(s)** This attribute focuses on what draws your followers to you and what purpose your leadership serves. Ask yourself two questions. First, do you challenge the existing thinking of your followers, or reinforce and build on their existing knowledge? Second, how are the group or groups of individuals you lead brought together by a common interest or responsibility? In most professional services contexts this will be a practice area or sector group under the leadership of a named individual.

As Joanna Worby's case study (introduced in the overview of the Self Leadership section) reveals, professionals who take on senior leadership roles typically find themselves leading professionals who possess knowledge and skills outside the leader's own domain expertise. In this scenario respect is gained and trust built through leadership capability rather than by demonstrating superior technical knowledge, as it might be when managing a junior colleague on a client matter.

A step further along the continuum are groups brought together by a particular outcome rather than topic. You might lead a division, business unit, or firm containing a mix of different practitioners. For example, some firms are increasingly bringing together multidisciplinary practices to offer clients integrated solutions on issues such as risk, reputation management, innovation or cyber security.

## Attribute 4: horizon

**Short term – medium term – long term – over the horizon – the unknown** Although the precise timeframes associated with each of the above definitions may vary, they are likely to be related to your leadership vision and strategy. Do you have a term-limited leadership role or are you able to take a more long-term view? What is the timeframe for your firm's strategic planning cycle? The difference between the first four time horizons is as much about certainty of outcome as it is about timescale.

The final term – 'the unknown' – is about leading in a context where it is necessary to challenge the status quo and to take a more radical view of how you want to change your firm for the future. Whereas leaders operating to known time horizons typically work from today forward (ie a three-year vision), leading in the unknown is about looking at potential future scenarios and working backwards from that point.

## Attribute 5: driver

**Employees – clients – business – self** To be successful your leadership responsibilities must come first, they are not a secondary task. It is important to take control over your personal leadership progression by thinking about which type of leadership you are most interested in and which type provides the best fit for you. Evaluate your leadership potential using three drivers – enjoyment, strengths and impact – against the four elements of the Leadership Triangle (business, clients, people and self).

It is important to ask yourself what type of leadership you enjoy most and what relative weight you would assign to each. One way to do this is to think about how you spend your time and the type of tasks that you naturally gravitate towards. For example, if a quarter of an hour window opened up in your diary, how would you use the time? Would you go to speak to your team? Would you use it to call a client? Would you review how you had led a meeting earlier in the day? Or would you use it to review the firm's latest financial data?

It is also important to understand where your strengths lie. Sometimes they will align with the areas you enjoy and sometimes there may be differences. Leaders understand they need to have a balanced focus on business, client, people and self leadership in order to maximize their leadership impact, but where they might have most impact is likely to change at different points in their leadership journey.

As far as possible, try to take an objective view. How do others in the firm assess your strengths and weaknesses? Insights from 360-degree appraisals can be particularly helpful here in gaining a fair picture of how others evaluate your leadership potential.

By mapping out your leadership profile against these three drivers (enjoyment, strengths and impact) you might identify gaps between how you score for each driver. Spend some time considering these gaps: it will help you consciously to choose your next leadership role, or to identify a development opportunity that will strengthen one or more of your leadership attributes.

As Nick Holt, former managing partner of KLegal and now a partner of SR Search, a specialist legal recruitment firm, identifies, the best leaders have a realistic view of their own potential and their limitations:

> Some people want to take on wide-ranging leadership responsibilities while others are perfectly happy just taking one element of their profession and focusing on it. There are some partners who are phenomenally good client people but who are poor business managers. We have all seen people who clients love, but who are not good with their people. It is important to know where your strengths and weaknesses are, what

your aspirations require them to be and to be honest with yourself about whether there is alignment, whether there are gaps and if so, whether you have the appetite to bridge them.

## Attribute 6: style

**Authoritative – directive – participative – inspirational – laissez-faire**
Leadership style refers to the way you behave as a leader and how others in your firm might characterize your leadership behaviour. We identify five broad styles of leadership commonly found in professional firms:

- Authoritative – leaders who take full control, giving little or no responsibility or authority to other people in their firm.

- Directive – leaders who set clear objectives, policies and processes for people in their firm and ensure that their expectations are clearly understood.

- Participative – leaders who invite input from people in their firm, factoring in multiple viewpoints when making decisions.

- Inspirational – leaders who motivate their team by creating a shared vision and lead by example in their words and actions.

- Laissez-faire – leaders who are hands-off and delegate most or all of their responsibilities to other people in their firm.

Leadership style isn't fixed in stone, nor is there one ideal style you should try to replicate at all times. Most people are adaptive and able to deploy the most appropriate style to suit the situation at hand. Look back through your diary over the last month and map the interactions where you have had to take on a leadership role. What kind of leadership style did you adopt and was that the optimum style to match the situation?

It is important to reflect on your leadership style to identify potential leadership blind spots. For example, if you are most comfortable at the inspirational end of the continuum, and you find yourself parachuted into a critical project or client engagement that is going wrong, could you honestly be comfortable deploying a more authoritative style?

When you have completed the personal leadership dimensions map you will have a better developed sense of yourself as a leader, including where your strengths lie and where you need to make changes to prepare yourself for the leadership role you want in the future. After you have completed the diagnostic, take a step back and consider the following questions:

- What does the leadership map say about you as a leader?
- What kind of leadership role would suit your strengths?
- What are your leadership blind spots that might reduce your future effectiveness as a leader?
- How should you adapt your leadership attributes to align better with the strategic challenges and opportunities facing your firm?

As we have said before there is no ideal leadership model to aspire to: two leaders, both successful within their own contexts, may have personal leadership maps that look very different. However, in our experience, successful leaders share two common traits: resilience and self-motivation. The ability to keep going when times get tough, as they inevitably will do at some point, cannot be underestimated. Tim Dixon-Phillip, co-founder of consultancy firm Service Reality and former sales and marketing director at EY, agrees:

> As a leader resilience is key. Leaders should have a support network, either an external coach or a buddy they keep to themselves. Some people, not many though, are relentless optimists who are just always 'half full' in attitude but they are very rare. Leaders need to recognize that much of their role in a professional services firm is about motivating others and, therefore, you need to stay motivated yourself. I think a lot of heads of department don't grasp that. They actually just revert to management rather than leadership. They do the easy stuff – the reporting or the meetings – but actually don't grasp the motivational role, perhaps because they haven't looked to get support with their own motivation.

## Map your routes into leadership roles

Unlike corporate organizations where the paths to leadership are well-trodden and better mapped, there are numerous routes that people in professional firms can follow to become leaders. Some leaders find their firm pulls them through the progression to leader: they may be identified as a future star performer and therefore loaded with training, coaching and a structured development programme. At the other end of the spectrum continuum there are self-driven people who have actively decided to pursue leadership and proactively source opportunities to develop their skills and experiences. It is important not to confuse drive with pushiness and see driven leaders as a negative; having clear aspirations and being able to articulate them, if done in the right way, is a positive attribute for leaders to possess.

There is also a third way on the continuum between pull and push: peer-selection. This is common in professional partnerships where a non-hierarchical group selects its leader to become a 'first amongst equals'. In this model, leaders most often emerge as the people identified by colleagues to have the best balance of leadership potential along with internal status and respect.

Whatever the route, it is important that aspiring leaders develop the right skills and experiences needed on their journey towards leadership. Nick Holt contrasts the corporate approach to leadership development, which tends to be more structured, with the traditional approach in professional firms which tends to be more ad hoc:

> How do you develop a future leader? My experience of corporates is that they are far better at rotating people around roles that will help to develop their leadership potential. People are given exposure for a couple of years in one business unit before being rotated around, or they are given experience working in a different geography. That doesn't really happen in most professional firms. As a future chief executive in a corporate you may be given the opportunity to run an overseas office but in a law firm you are a banking lawyer or a corporate lawyer and that's what you do. You might go abroad for three years, but there isn't the same diversity of experience.
>
> I have found that successful leaders often proactively seek opportunities if their firm isn't forthcoming in providing them. They are the people who have a hunger for knowledge and want to learn about the business of law, rather than the practice of law. These people have often done two or three different jobs, have been at two or three different law firms, or have been in-house as a client, which allows them to pick up vital skills about the business of law along the way.

Routes to leadership are also determined by the extent to which the leadership selection process is systematic or not. Many leaders feel that their progression has been driven by circumstance: they were in the right place, or perhaps the wrong place, at the right time. They may have found themselves in a project or team that, for whatever reason, suddenly had a leadership void, or perhaps they were working on a client account or matter that suddenly grew and so required a more structured approach to leadership. These situations are uncontrolled and unplanned.

For more controlled routes into leadership there is more likely to be either a career path that involves a rise at a natural pace or one that has been, for whatever reason, accelerated. The majority of professional firms still choose their leaders through partnership elections. These are structured processes that can be deeply imbued with personal politics and factionalism. As a result of this, as Nick Holt observes, the most suited candidates don't always rise to the top or even put their name into the ring for a leadership position: 'When firms have managing partner elections, you often find that many people don't put themselves forward, despite being well-suited candidates. It can be a bit diffident and self-effacing. Personal credibility, trust, network and influence matter in these situations almost as much as track record and future vision, perhaps even more so.'

There are more insights about how best to navigate the internal politics of professional firms throughout the People Leadership section of this handbook.

Plotting out two determining factors of your route to leadership – the primary mover in the selection process and the circumstances of the selection process – reveals that there are six broad routes to leadership in professional firms (see Figure 10.3). Each of these routes has different characteristics as we outline below.

## 1 Accidental

Leaders who, due to circumstances beyond their control (for example, early retirement or sudden departure of a colleague), have found themselves occupying a leadership position. They may or may not have the skills, experience or confidence for the situation they find themselves in. They may not even have the support of the people around them, particularly if they are perceived to be unsuited for the leadership role.

**Figure 10.3**   The six routes to leadership in professional firms

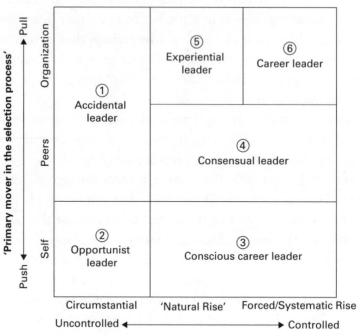

**2 Opportunist**

Leaders who have actively decided to seek out leadership opportunities and focus their attention on activities that help them to reach this goal. Opportunist leaders will often be quite open about their desires, aspirations and goals, but may find that their desire for leadership responsibility clouds their judgement about which roles are best suited to their skills. If they are managed in the right way, opportunist leaders can be directed towards more suitable roles.

**3 Conscious Career**

Leaders who make a conscious decision to lead, and have sought out opportunities to develop their skills and capabilities and who take on relevant experiences that will make them better leaders in the long term. They will likely be open about this and will be able to articulate what they want to achieve and why. Typically, conscious career leaders leverage the more formal approaches available to them in order to further their professional development.

**4 Consensual**

Leaders who are cited as 'natural born leaders' by their peers, but aren't actively looking for leadership roles. Very few people fit this category. Although they might not be looking for leadership, they are often the best candidates for a particular context or time (for example to lead the turnaround of an underperforming team or to lead the launch of a new service proposition) and are usually selected by their peers on the basis of a track record.

**5 Experiential**

Leaders who have experienced a paced and managed rise to leadership during which they will have taken steps to develop their skills, capabilities and experiences in order to equip themselves to take on increasing levels of responsibility. The majority of these steps will have been incremental in nature, rather than part of a conscious long-term plan to achieve leadership.

**6 Career**

Leaders who will likely have been 'pulled' through a more forced growth in leadership skills, often because their leadership potential has been highlighted by others in the firm. While they will have a depth of professional experience, in comparison to other types of leader, they may have a relatively wide but shallow blend of leadership experiences. Other professionals may see them as occupying positions of leadership because of a fast-track process rather than professional competence.

Any leadership career will probably involve moving between two or more of these routes. The important thing for aspiring leaders – and current leaders looking for a new challenge – is to identify which route or routes you might be on at any point in time and to understand whether that will generate the kind of progression you are looking for. If not, you might need to reassess whether you have the right balance of skills and experiences and where there are leadership blind spots that you need to plug.

**CASE STUDY** The importance of forward-looking leadership – the view from a sales and marketing director

For leaders it is not about doing more but often about doing things differently that can have the biggest impact. For Tim Dixon-Phillip, former sales and marketing director at EY, who now runs his own firm Service Reality, this means that leaders need to ensure that they are forward-looking and not dwelling on the past.

It can be tempting for leaders to focus attention on where the firm has been rather than the future. Although leaders need to learn from past experience, conversations with colleagues should be focused on how people plan to use their time over the next month and how they will help to further the firm's strategic goals. For Tim, this means apparently simple things, such as celebrating the behaviours you are looking for in your teams, which can be very important. 'If a team has achieved three new appointments in the next month with some really good targets, this needs to be celebrated,' he says.

'In my experience leaders need to force themselves to look at their agenda when they meet with others in the firm,' says Tim. 'If it is all going to be about the WIP, the lock-up and the chargeable hours, it can become a pretty turgid conversation. A more interesting question to ask of others might be: how on earth did you manage to get a meeting with the FD or General Counsel at that company? What did you do to get the meeting and how we can capitalize on it now that we are building that relationship?'

Shining a light on best practice activity and taking a more future-looking perspective can lead to much more engaging internal meetings with more interaction, creativity and connections being made between people and opportunities. Given the amount of time and energy professional firms invest in meetings, as a leader you need to ensure that every minute of this time is being put to effective use and that people are focused, engaged and aligned with purpose.

Leaders who establish a forward-looking leadership approach find it easier to cascade this mindset throughout their firm. 'What I saw work well was for every partner to have a coaching session, one hour a month, with their head of department, and every head of department had to have a coaching session with their line up,' says Tim. 'These sessions were only an hour, but it helped to instil a culture where people were goal-focused and were regularly given constructive feedback and challenge.'

**SUMMARY**   Top tips for assessing and developing your
leadership potential

### Evaluate your leadership attributes honestly

All leaders have strengths and weaknesses but the best leaders reflect
openly and honestly on what their strengths and weaknesses are. Use
the Personal leadership dimensions map to plot out your leadership
attributes and to identify where your leadership blind spots might be.
When assessing your attributes think about how you behave in a range
of leadership scenarios (business, client and people leadership) and how
your peers and team members would describe your leadership style.

### Invest regularly and consistently in your self leadership

Schedule an hour in your diary at regular intervals to review your
leadership attributes and progress. Professionals typically review
objectives and goals before performance reviews but don't often take
the time to self-reflect on personal development throughout the year. It
is important to focus on leadership progress with the same rigour as on
professional competencies and technical development.

### Identify your leadership fit

Leadership comes in many guises. Different leadership opportunities suit
people with different mixes of skills and experiences. Ask yourself what kind
of leadership role you would most enjoy and challenge yourself to articulate
why: where are you likely to be most successful? Pursuing leadership for its
own sake may lead you down a blind alley or set you up for failure.

### Take ownership of your development path

Once you know what leadership path will help you fulfil your leadership
potential, you need to look at how you can go about achieving this
goal. Actively seek out a portfolio of opportunities that mix planned and
serendipitous opportunities. Be able and willing to share your experiences
and aspirations to allow others time to help you find the opportunities you
want. Even in firms with structured leadership progression opportunities, it
is important to take ownership of your own leadership development.

### Think about leadership as a long-term goal

Leadership is more like a decathlon than a 100-metre sprint. You should
give yourself plenty of time and space to develop in the many areas that

are going to be critical to your success. As part of your reflection time, consider your aspirations in the context of external factors such as the economic climate: leadership in a growing market requires a different set of skills to leadership in a downturn. Consider the maturity of your skills, your network and the alignment of your self-perception with that of others, and how you might overcome any negative perceptions within your firm about your preparedness to lead.

# Capability: how to develop the skills, competencies and experiences to be a successful leader    11

The transition from being a professional to running a professional services business is not an easy undertaking. As George Bull, senior tax partner at accountancy firm RSM, rightly notes, this transition requires a step change in both skills and personal outlook:

> Taking on a leadership role requires a new set of capabilities but it is also a mindset shift. If somebody's perspective has shifted they will know where they are strong, where they are weak and where they have gaps they need to remedy. As a professional moves up through their firm, they realize that being a good accountant, a good architect, a good lawyer, is actually no more than a prerequisite to get to the leadership starting block. A lot of people are hampered because they don't have a business-like view of the business they operate in. So when it's their turn to run parts of the business they are not well-equipped to do that.

In our experience the leaders who have found this transition easiest have been the ones who have consciously made time to reflect on the skills and experiences they need to acquire to become better leaders. In this chapter we consider what those leadership capabilities are (what we will refer to as a leadership 'concept of operations') and how successful leaders create and sustain a leadership profile within their firm. Leaders who are self-aware are often equipped to align their leadership capabilities with the particular strategic context of their firm and, hence, are able to maximize their impact as a leader when setting strategic direction and overseeing its implementation.

# Leadership profile: what do you want to be known for?

Think of a leader you have worked with during your career. How would you describe them? What made them effective as a leader? Successful leaders typically deliver business performance in a way that fits with their organization's values, mission and strategy, while adopting a leadership style and approach that fits credibly with their personal attributes. It is this personal leadership profile that is often most recognizable or memorable when somebody is asked to describe a leader.

A person's leadership profile is a patchwork of the way they act and communicate (either overtly or subconsciously) and how they manifest their personal values during interactions with colleagues. As Joanna Worby, managing partner of law firm Brachers, says building a credible personal leadership profile in your firm allows you to leverage greater influence over how others behave: 'Your personal profile both within the firm and outside is really important because at the end of the day everybody looks to you to lead by example.'

In the previous chapter we asked you to consider your leadership attributes against six specific criteria. Using those criteria as a foundation, now think about how you would define your overall approach to leadership. To begin to define your own leadership profile, ask yourself the following three questions:

1 What are my core values?

2 How would I like to be known by others (both clients and those who I work with)?

3 How would I define success from a business performance perspective?

Everybody has core values, but often in a work environment they can be subordinated to the organization's values. Successful leaders inhabit a mindset that blends together the organization's values with their own, rather than seeing these two sets of values as a trade-off. The difficulty in articulating personal core values is that they are often hardwired into our very being and are by nature subconscious. If you are struggling to define your core values, the following questions might help spur your thinking – keep interrogating your responses until you get to an answer that feels authentic to you:

- When have you felt happy about a decision, in a work context or otherwise? What was it about that decision that made you feel happy?

- When have you made a decision, in a work context or otherwise, that you felt was the wrong decision? What was it that drove that feeling?

- Think about a decision that you have made that you felt passionate about. What was it that underpinned or drove the passion?

- When you read a newspaper, what is it that drives the emotions that you feel when reading a particular article?

Although our core values are hardwired into our persona, what other people experience and see in us can be different. Unless we consciously think about and talk about how we would like to be perceived by others, then it's likely that the context we find ourselves in will disproportionately drive the perceptions that others have of us. The reality that others experience may well undermine our personal brand and often appear inconsistent, unpredictable and changeable. As Joanna Worby notes, the more visible you can be as a leader, the better that people will understand your leadership profile:

> I think having a personal profile and a network is important whatever stage you are in your leadership journey. You have got to mix with your peers because that's how you learn and that's how they learn about you. As a business owner or director you really need to understand and learn about the challenges of people on your team, so that you can understand how best to help them and they can understand what help you can provide as a leader and the impact you will have on their future career.

Write down how you would like to be perceived by others around you in your firm. For example, do you want to be seen as a leader who always says yes to clients, or would you like to be seen as someone who drives a robust but fair deal? Do you want your team to feel that you've always got time for them no matter what the issue, or would you like to be viewed as supportive yet slightly removed from the team?

Asking the people you trust what their views are of you may feel uncomfortable, but in our experience successful leaders proactively create more opportunities to ask for feedback. This feedback could be built into 'business as usual' moments. For example, after a key meeting try asking a selection of attendees: how do you think the meeting went? Is there anything that I could have done differently to get a better outcome?

However, having a strong and credible leadership profile is all well and good but it is only the foundation for successful leadership. To achieve real change and influence in your firm, your leadership profile needs to have impact. Leaders in professional services firms often define their leadership impact using a basket of measures across the business, people and client elements of the Leadership Triangle, the balance varying depending on what they want to achieve, how and why. Successful leaders know that performance is driven by a mix of financial metrics, client satisfaction and employee engagement. More details about appropriate metrics to use for measuring business, client and people performance can be found in the respective sections of this handbook.

# Develop your leadership skills, competencies and experiences

Most organizations have their own approaches to learning and development but alongside that you need to consider your personal leadership development strategy. In Chapter 7, on People Leadership, we explored the concept of the commercially savvy professional, who is able to provide clients with a broader commercial outlook, not just a technical solution to problems. This concept is even more important in the context of leadership success because as somebody leading a firm, or a team within a professional services firm, you need to develop a blend of commercial competencies. This blend is likely to encompass competencies such as strategic decision-making, communications, and analytical thinking, along with a better understanding of other professional areas that are critical to your organization such as finance, business development or project management.

When building your leadership development strategy it is, therefore, important to ensure that you focus on an appropriate balance of competencies based on your leadership route, experience level and the leadership attributes identified in the previous chapter. It is crucial to challenge yourself to make sure that you move outside the comfort zone of technical professional skills into blended leadership skills. As Nick Holt argues, gaining a broad perspective early on in your career can help to accelerate your transition into leadership:

> My transition from practising partner to leader was helped because
> I had spent some time out of private practice. I spent nine years as
> an in-house lawyer, including three years running a business where I
> stopped being a lawyer and ran a stockbroking business in Hong Kong.
> When I went back to being a lawyer there was a perception that I had,
> somehow, better business acumen because I had been in a business,
> wasn't frightened of numbers and was able to think strategically. As a
> result of that experience I found myself taking on things that a managing partner typically does because other people don't want to do it. If
> I had stayed as a lawyer in private practice I might not have acquired
> any of these skills because very few firms regard it as their task to equip
> people with those skills. What is most important to them, if you are a
> lawyer, is how many chargeable hours you're doing.

The skills you need to develop as a leader can be honed in different ways. The nature of the interventions that you will use for various skills will be different. For example, while you might adopt a traditional formal learning approach for improving project management capabilities, you might decide to undergo a tailored and interactive media skills workshop to enhance your communication skills. Increasingly, leaders will have to look at the challenge laterally to develop the broad portfolio of competencies needed.

Coaching is another area that can be very beneficial at various stages of your leadership journey. Historically, coaching has been viewed by some firms as something that is provided when a person is underperforming but today many more firms recognize that business coaching targeted at high-performing individuals can help them to achieve even more, just as sports coaching does with elite athletes. As Kimberly Bradshaw, managing director of HR services at accountancy firm Buzzacott, notes, coaching can play a powerful role in unlocking leadership potential:

> I found the transition to leadership can sometimes be quite lonely. As somebody leading a practice that has experienced rapid growth, I encountered lots of challenges: hiring quickly to respond to client demand, trying to turn one-off projects into repeat business and trying to meet profit targets to ensure our growth is sustainable. It has been an ever-changing evolution on a day-by-day basis, so the need to be very adaptable and flexible has been paramount. That is where a coach has really helped. For me a coach is a strategic thinking partner, somebody who is by my side on the journey who gives me an opportunity to reflect and who helps me to understand that I am capable of dealing with the various challenges on my agenda at any one time.

Unlike a mentor who will actively help you to make linkages and connections, a coach will work with you to unlock solutions that are within the abilities, resources and competencies that you already have. Whereas mentors will typically come from within your sector or organization and have direct experience, coaches will more likely be external and may not have direct experience of your sector. It is this independence that can be very valuable for a developing leader.

In order to find opportunities to develop and practise leadership skills and competencies, it is very important that your learning and development is choreographed within the broader development of your role and responsibilities. Although any new role will have its own learning curve, the leadership learning curve can be particularly steep. Having to back-fill too many skills means that, as a leader, you will be less than well-prepared for the challenges you face during your most vulnerable period. Ensuring that you have a burst of learning and development in advance of any transition to leadership should be a key part of any promotion discussion or performance review within your firm. At the transition point to leadership, coaching can be a valuable addition to focused training to help you step back from situations and, with the help of an impartial supporter, find your way to workable solutions to your challenges.

# Maximize your impact through an adaptive leadership style

Leaders who have developed a self-awareness of their leadership capabilities find they are able to adapt their leadership style in different scenarios to drive optimum performance. These leaders are consequently able to deliver performance in almost any scenario. This kind of leadership adaption can occur at the macro level (for example, using a different style between core business areas and innovative new business areas) and the micro level (for example, changing leadership style depending on the performance level of a project or the relative experience of the people involved).

As George Bull notes, leaders also need to adapt their style according to the risk appetite of the firm, or the risk level of a particular project or team:

> Leaders need to think carefully about how they manage their tolerance of risk. In a professional services context even ambitious leaders need to accommodate themselves to the risk appetite of their organization. Many professional firms are naturally risk-averse and this aversion can translate into very good management of risk, both in terms of their own business and also looking after clients. But leaders also need to recognize that if risk-aversion is the brake in a car, people don't always drive with their foot on the brake; there is a clutch and the accelerator and sometimes it is important to go more quickly and sometimes it is important to move more slowly. Leaders need to give partners in their firm a holistic view of risk to understand when is the most appropriate time to move at what speed.

Think about this scenario: you have a regular meeting to review a project and are under pressure with a wide range of things that need to be delivered. You have only five or ten minutes of preparation time in which to review the actions from the last meeting and perhaps to sketch out the key issues and what you would like to see come from the meeting. What leadership style will you adopt to generate the outcome you want for the meeting? How will this leadership style manifest itself in the way you speak and behave, what you say and how you interact with other people?

Very few people take the time to actively consider their leadership style in scenarios like this. In our experience, a simple framework can make thinking about leadership style more systematic and move it towards being habitual. Successful leaders train themselves to block out space in their busy diaries, either once a day, or on a meeting by meeting basis, to create time to think about leadership style.

The leadership style mapper, see Figure 11.1, covers a number of areas that will help you to think through how to adapt your leadership style to suit the needs of different scenarios. It can be filled in either before key meetings, or as an aide memoire to help you quickly think through some of the key aspects of your approach in a given scenario.

The example in Figure 11.1 has been completed using the scenario of a performance review with an underperforming team in which you have to make a decision about the way forward. The template gives details of the scenario including the background, stakeholders and the key decisions and/or outcomes required. Once you understand these important contextual factors it is possible to think about how you want the meeting to go and how you might need to adapt your leadership style to achieve that result. We have clustered a range of leadership attributes into four categories over which you can map your profile: your role, setting the environment, style of progress and decision-making style.

To help plot your leadership profile against the attributes on the leadership style mapper, you might find it helpful to ask yourself the following questions:

- Lead/follow: are you going to lead or will you allow another person to lead with your role to support and review?

- Proximity: do you want to give the impression that you are one of the team or an outsider?

- Emotiveness: are you unflappable and steady, or do you want to demonstrate passion and emotion?

- Energy levels: how active do you want other people to be? A high energy environment might involve consciously going round the table asking for views or using brainstorming activities.

**Figure 11.1**  Leadership style mapper

---

**BACKGROUND**

| Description of activity/meeting/interaction: | **Key stakeholders** |
| --- | --- |
| Monthly review meeting of department financial performance – currently underperforming year-to-date targets | Greg Pepper (COO) |
| | Bill Smith (Finance Director) |
| | Steve Jones (Operations Manager) |
| | Dave Lloyd (Senior Associate) |

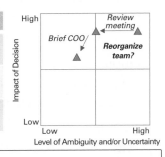

Relative Importance

Client / Business / Employees Self

**KEY OUTCOMES/DECISIONS**

| | **Decision/outcome** |
| --- | --- |
| 1 | Is recovery plan for drift from year-to-date targets in place with clear attributable and achievable actions? |
| 2 | Robust review of opportunities pipeline |
| 3 | Reorganize team? Options: leave as is/change team lead/ fold into team B |

High

Impact of Decision

Brief COO / Review meeting

Reorganize team?

Low

Low          High
Level of Ambiguity and/or Uncertainty

---

**What does success look like?**
Acceptable recovery plan agreed which can be briefed to COO and then implemented

---

**MY LEADERSHIP STYLE**

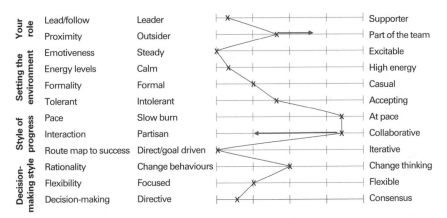

| | | |
| --- | --- | --- |
| **Your role** | Lead/follow | Leader — Supporter |
| | Proximity | Outsider — Part of the team |
| **Setting the environment** | Emotiveness | Steady — Excitable |
| | Energy levels | Calm — High energy |
| | Formality | Formal — Casual |
| | Tolerant | Intolerant — Accepting |
| **Style of progress** | Pace | Slow burn — At pace |
| | Interaction | Partisan — Collaborative |
| | Route map to success | Direct/goal driven — Iterative |
| **Decision-making style** | Rationality | Change behaviours — Change thinking |
| | Flexibility | Focused — Flexible |
| | Decision-making | Directive — Consensus |

- Formality: do you want to set a formal agenda with clear roles, or approach things in a more free-flowing and creative way?

- Tolerant: how tolerant will you be of participants deviating from the stated purpose, agenda or objective? In a scenario where you want to encourage creativity, for example, you are likely to want an element of tolerance.

- Pace: how quickly do you want to move towards your desired objectives or goals?

- Interaction: do you need to challenge others from a personal or organizational perspective, or are you looking to work with them to find a solution?

- Route map to success: is there a clear and obvious solution where a direct approach can be used or is the solution less clear? The degree of clarity will influence how you go about getting buy-in to any solutions. Scenarios where the route map is unclear may benefit from a more iterative approach.

- Rationality: do you need to change people's thinking in order to change their behaviours, or do you need to change their behaviour to bring about a change in mindset?

- Flexibility: is there reasonable clarity on the decision which just needs to be tested or is the outcome in doubt and therefore flexible?

- Decision-making: do you need to be the focal point and the decision-maker, or are you looking to create consensus?

In reality, these attributes are not binary, each involves shades of grey. Sometimes it may be necessary to start in one position to make a point and then moderate your leadership style at a later point in a meeting to reach the desired outcome. This is indicated in Figure 11.1 with an arrow on the 'Interaction' and 'Proximity' attributes.

If you record your thoughts in writing, it can be helpful to review them following your interaction with others. In the example in Figure 11.1, an honest self-assessment after the review meeting may reveal that it was unwise to try to reach a decision at such a fast pace, and that it might have been fruitful to slow the pace of the discussion down in order to convey a sense that, as a leader, you are open to dialogue and new ideas. The mapper can therefore become a learning tool helping you to identify where there are gaps between your leadership aspirations and reality, and where you might need to focus your attention as part of your leadership development plan to further enhance your leadership capabilities.

# Leadership capabilities in practice: your leadership 'concept of operations'

In our experience successful leaders have a very distinct, almost systematic, approach to how they demonstrate their leadership impact. When approaching a new role or responsibility, for example, they may have an approach that tests and aligns people with their way of working. We call this approach to putting leadership capabilities into practice the leadership 'concept of operations'. It comprises five building blocks, as outlined in Figure 11.2: purpose, environment, performance, responsibilities and mechanisms.

## Purpose

Achieving clarity of a common purpose is fundamental to the success of any firm. As a leader it is your role to provide clarity, understanding and buy-in to this shared purpose. Don't assume that everybody in your firm is in the same place or will remain in alignment over time. It is important to test this, not just early on in your role, but to continue to test decisions, options and progress against the common purpose. That is why we place this capability at the core of the concept of operations.

**Figure 11.2**   Your leadership concept of operations

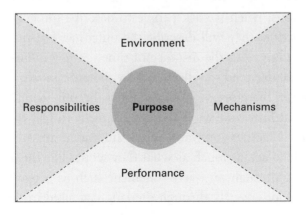

It is important to link purpose back to strategy but not to let it become so rigid that the tactical options are blinkered by the strategic view. As discussed in the Business Leadership chapters, a good strategic purpose should define the ultimate goal and the boundaries but not necessarily constrain the route for getting there. The need for purpose is hardwired into us as human beings and fundamental to most human activity; being able to articulate it and create a common understanding and buy-in is a success differentiator because it gives us a reason to be a part of a group or team.

## Environment

One of the differences between leadership and management is the environment that the leader or manager creates. Management is about driving performance through order, stability and consistency, largely focused on the present moment and the short term. Leadership, on the other hand, is about driving performance through change, influence and flexibility, and so is usually more focused on the future and the longer term. From these two high-level descriptions, it is easy to see that the environment that each of these approaches needs to create is different.

So much of business, particularly in a professional services firm, is a social activity, with success driven in a large part by human interactions both within your firm and with clients, intermediaries and other third parties. Leadership, by its very nature, is a very social activity too. Yet too often conversations about business fail to consider the emotional dynamic. We see this reluctance often in key business interactions, such as negotiations; when we ask people to describe the negotiation just after completion, they will describe the outcomes but rarely describe how it felt. Only with the distance of time – a few months or a year later – will people tend to reflect on how the process felt.

As a leader, therefore, it is important to become comfortable with talking about how you want the environment to feel for people, as much as the outcomes you want. Successful leaders articulate how they want people to act, as much as what they would like them to achieve. This may be through an overt statement such as a team charter or set of values, or covertly through the language used to describe their purpose. Further details about how to drive high performance among your people can be found in Chapter 8 of the People Leadership section.

## Performance

Leaders need to measure performance to help people understand whether the actions they are taking match the direction, and pace, required to achieve the common purpose. The performance evaluation framework that you put in place, therefore, has to support this, providing confidence to those around you that their actions are in alignment. As you take on larger leadership roles, where perhaps you need to evaluate performance across a whole firm, this becomes even more important. As George Bull notes, managing partners need to understand that the way they evaluate and drive performance is likely to be different in different parts of their firm:

> The management team must understand that if they have different business streams making profits in different ways then those business streams have to be managed and evaluated differently. This is vitally important. For example, lock-up might be an extremely important measure in private client work, but if you're in transactional work you're probably going to be more interested in other parameters.

In our experience an effective performance evaluation framework meets four basic criteria. It is:

- Layered – it uses a range of metrics to measure performance from different perspectives and over different timeframes. It is common for firms to bring these metrics together into a balanced scorecard to give a one-page representation of performance which can be easily communicated to the firm.

- Transparent – it is important to be open about positive progress and any progress that is sub-optimal so that people have confidence that they are moving in the right direction and know when to change course.

- Flexible – an openness to adapt the evaluation approach is a critical skill for successful leaders because it demonstrates that they are listening to both the people around them and the wider environment. Laying out a strategic vision is like telling a story: a direction of travel should be established at the outset, which will evolve as the strategy is implemented. The performance evaluation framework will need to evolve to support the change with an adjustment in metrics or targets accordingly.

- Linked with incentives – people in the firm should be able to see a clear link between how performance is evaluated and how they are rewarded and incentivized. Although the shared purpose may be optimum for the firm collectively, some people may perceive misalignment with what is best for them as individuals. Therefore, some incentivization or nudges may be required to reach desired outcomes.

One of the most effective ways of maintaining performance as a leader is to tap into the competitive spirit of people in your firm. This can be as simple as celebrating performance of high-achievers with recognition or soft reward. Tim Dixon-Phillip explains why this approach works well:

> One of the things that I have seen heads of department doing really well is using the natural competitive nature of professionals to drive increased performance. One approach is to publish league tables or traffic lights for key accounts: we gave key accounts, each of which were led by a named individual, a green traffic light if we thought it was progressing well and we were going to hit our targets, an amber if it was a cause of concern and a red if it was completely off track. Nobody wants a red. Tapping into that peer group pressure can be an effective way to motivate partners. Alongside that peer pressure though, you have to make sure you are visibly celebrating small victories so that people see there is a benefit in aiming to be top of the league table.

## Responsibilities

A key aspect of leadership is ensuring that there is clarity over the roles and responsibilities within the organization or team that are required to achieve your common purpose. Clarity of responsibilities will ensure that information and knowledge is created, shared and used consistently and that the people best equipped to make decisions do so with the best insights and support. Joanna Worby explains the benefit she gained from creating clear lines of responsibility and accountability at Brachers:

> I have spent a lot of time with all of our partners trying to show them that they are owners in the business, that they have responsibility and control, and that things don't happen because of one person, the leader. It is all about teamwork and if the leader disappeared tomorrow for any reason, the firm must go on. So it is vital for them to know what we're

trying to do and to throw their heart into it, because we are all busy. The learning for me has been to just keep bringing our strategy, vision and purpose to the top of the agenda every time. We have changed the governance structure of the firm so that every time the strategy board meets it looks at what progress the executive has made in delivering on the strategy, and so is holding us completely accountable.

One technique that gives clarity to roles and responsibilities is the RACI matrix. This can be used to outline who is Responsible, Accountable, Consulted and Informed for major decisions and activities within the firm. The discussions required to create and maintain a RACI matrix can be as valuable as the RACI matrix itself because it brings to the surface an opportunity to talk about how to align people better with the firm's purpose and environment.

We often find that a proper RACI analysis can help to free up the time of senior stakeholders in a firm, who often feel they are overlooked when strategic decisions are taken. It is not uncommon to find influential partners trying to insert themselves unnecessarily into the decision-making process as a responsible person, which can disrupt progress and risks derailing decisions. Being clear with these individuals up front that they will be consulted or informed can resolve the issue of excessive partner time being spent on convoluted decision-making.

## Mechanisms

This final capability in the leadership concept of operations relates to communication mechanisms that you can deploy to drive forward a leadership strategy. As Figure 11.3 illustrates, there is a wide spectrum of possible mechanisms at your disposal. Despite this, it is not uncommon to find leaders getting stuck in a rut of communicating in the same way year in year out, and therefore missing a trick to increase the impact of their communications.

Ask yourself what is the most appropriate method of communication to convey the messages you want, to the audience you want, at the level of detail you want. In our experience, leaders miss a trick in not communicating more with their colleagues: important messages have to be repeated several times before they are typically understood by other people.

**Figure 11.3** Mechanisms at your disposal

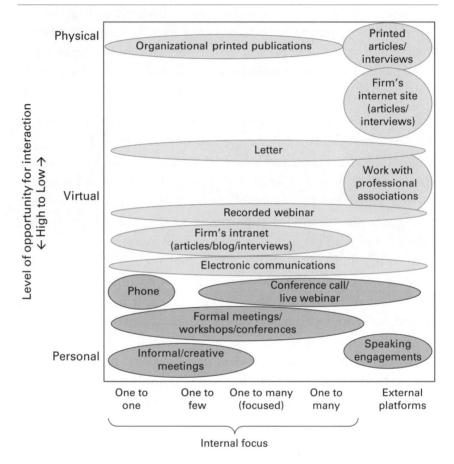

**CASE STUDY** Performance measurement – so much more than the financials at Arup

One definition of business success could be picking the right opportunities and delivering them well. In the world of professional services, performance is often measured in billable hours, revenue per fee-earner, or profit per equity partner. These are important measures, particularly for delivering financial performance, but they don't tell the whole story of how a firm is performing.

A key element of the role of a leader is to set and maintain a strategic direction and then to ensure that course is carried through over time. This came to the surface in discussion with Ed Clark, director and building engineering group leader at the independent engineering and design consultancy firm Arup. 'You can measure profit on a project, that is fine,' says Ed, 'but how do you know that you are going in the right direction in other areas? While we don't have these measures written down, there are five things that we measure at the end of the project to see whether it was a successful project.'

Ed elaborates on his five measures, starting with profitability. 'You've got to make some money but, in a way, that is a by-product. If you get the other things right, financial performance should follow,' he says. The other measures used include areas such as social purpose, technical excellence, relationships and employee satisfaction. 'Fundamentally, a project has to have a social purpose. So whether we are planning a new school or HS2 we have to be happy that we are actually improving the world somehow through that project,' he says.

'There has got to be a technical story, an innovation or a degree of technical excellence that will make you proud of the project,' he adds. 'We want to come away with happy clients and happy collaborators, so the project as a vehicle has strengthened rather than weakened our relationship with collaborators. It has got to be, on balance, a positive experience for the team, so everyone on this side of the fence comes away having learnt something and can also feel proud of it.'

Ed cross-checks opportunities throughout their lifecycle against a number of the firm's core values and long-term aims (see the case study in Chapter 1 for more details about Arup's aims and values). He doesn't apply them as a dogmatic 'go, no-go gauge' but uses the firm's values to assess and guide opportunity development and delivery to ensure that, while there will inevitably be diversions from time to time, the long-term course is maintained.

---

**SUMMARY** Top tips for developing your leadership competencies and maximizing your impact

### Be clear about your personal leadership profile

Develop, test and hone your personal leadership profile to the point where you are comfortable with it, and can articulate it when prompted by others. It is important that this leadership profile aligns with your aspirations and feels authentic in terms of the way you speak and behave with others. At regular intervals reflect on whether you are living up to your personal profile and how you might need to adapt your focus to the particular leadership challenges of the moment.

### Plan out your leadership route map

It is critical to carry out an honest appraisal of your leadership skills, competencies and experience, mapping both where you are today and where you need to be. Think about your route in terms of the four elements of the Leadership Triangle – business, clients, people and self leadership – and what you need to do to achieve a balanced set of skills across each area. Ask yourself what mix of learning and development activities will help you move forward on your leadership route map: formal learning, experiential learning or social and peer learning.

### Push yourself outside your comfort zone to embrace new skills

As a leader you need to break out of the comfort zone of professional and technical skills development. Apply the same rigour to leadership skills development as you would to your professional competencies by allocating time for targeted skills development around your business and domain context, and personal leadership effectiveness.

### Prepare actively for key leadership interactions

Create time to prepare for meetings and other interactions where you put your leadership capabilities into practice. Balance how you use this designated preparation time to cover both what you want to achieve and how you plan to achieve it using the optimum leadership style to fit the matter in hand. No world class athlete would run a race without warming up if they want to win, so no leader should enter unprepared into important leadership interactions in their firm.

### Don't shy away from self-analysis and seeking feedback from others

Your leadership capabilities don't exist in a vacuum. Only by getting regular feedback from peers, employees and clients, whom you trust not to tell you what they think you want to hear, can you properly hone those skills over time. Sometimes there can be misalignment between how you want to be perceived as a leader and how others actually perceive you. Getting to grips with why these gaps exist and what you can do to plug them early on will help you to hone your leadership capabilities as effectively as possible.

# Balance: how to succeed as a leader without burning out

12

*Look at the journey on which newly appointed leaders embark. Once they are promoted their self-esteem initially receives an enormous boost. They then realize they can't cope, so self-esteem falls back. Typically, new leaders then copy what their predecessor did, which might work for a short period so their esteem goes back up, but then they find it drops again quickly afterwards because copying the strategies of their predecessors is not an authentic approach for them.*

*Leaders need to make the job their own. In my experience, it might take 18 months before self-esteem is on a steadily rising trend and somebody is actually doing the job on their own terms. I think that firms and new leaders should understand this 18-month curve because it is inexcusable in today's environment that there should be a hiatus of 18 months while a new person, who may have come up from within the firm, is finding their feet as a leader. It ought to be possible to compress that learning curve.*

GEORGE BULL, SENIOR TAX PARTNER AT RSM

One of the biggest issues any professional services leader faces is balancing all the demands on their time. Is it possible to combine running a business, motivating a team and keeping clients happy without burning out completely? The successful professional services leaders we interviewed prove the answer is yes, but only because they delegate properly and have strategies for managing their diary and prioritizing their time.

In the Business Leadership section, we saw that developing a strategic vision for your firm is only the start: to achieve success, you also have to invest time and effort in the implementation. The leadership strategy and personal leadership profile, discussed in the previous two chapters are no different: you need to use your time wisely to implement your personal leadership plan successfully. As you read through this chapter, reflect critically on where you are now: does the way you use your time currently set you up for success or failure?

Successful leaders may make the role look easy but that is usually far from the case. In talking to leaders within professional firms about the biggest challenges that they experience, particularly at the transition point into a leadership role, the following observations are commonplace:

- Suddenly, you are overwhelmed with what everyone else is struggling with and expected to magic up solutions to their problems.

- Your day becomes an endless series of 30 minute slots where, in each one, people look to you to provide them with answers and wisdom, on tap.

- The variety of focus becomes exponentially diverse. One minute you have to deliver client advice, the next minute you need to review monthly firm-wide accounts and then deal with a sudden personal team issue.

- It feels as though leadership is supplementary to the existing role and just added on top of all existing responsibilities.

As a leader, every day can feel like you are being swamped, bombarded and overwhelmed by an increasing set of demands from a diverse range of stakeholders. With the spotlight on you, others look to you for guidance and solutions to their problems. If not managed well the demands of leadership within a professional services firm can begin to feel relentless.

In this situation highly driven leaders can be their own worst enemy. Their desire to succeed makes them overly sensitive to external triggers. This sensitivity can cause them, certainly when they are relatively new to a leadership position, to swing between 'puffing their chest up' to drive forward issues with an almost arrogant confidence in order to demonstrate their strong leadership, and being overly cautious on issues that are straightforward because they may have over-interpreted a viewpoint or market signal as a result of subconscious biases. With experience, leaders can moderate these pendulous swings and find a more balanced approach to leadership problem-solving.

# Client work: to retain or not to retain, that is the question

Is leading a professional services firm a full-time role or is it possible to be an effective leader and continue to balance the commitments of client work? Does retaining a client-facing role make you a better-informed leader or distract you from the responsibilities of leadership? These questions are frequently asked by leaders and aspiring leaders throughout the professional services sector. In some cases the need to give up client work and a concern about what will happen after stepping down from a leadership role, prevents well-qualified candidates from putting their name forward for leadership positions in the first place. However, the experience of successful leaders suggests that a balance can be reached that will allow them to focus their time without jeopardizing their career.

Whether or not a leader steps down entirely from the demands of client work depends on the nature of the leadership role (whether it is a firm-wide managing partner role, or a head of practice area, for example), the size of the firm and how well the demands of leadership are understood within the culture of the firm. Although there is no absolute rule, the vast majority of professional services leaders reduce their chargeable hours targets, in most cases to zero, on taking on a firm-wide leadership role. Even heads of department or equivalent leadership roles typically spend a minority of their time on fee-earning work. Therefore, if you are somebody that has a passion for client work and would find it an anathema to give up fee-earning, then leadership may not be right for you.

Leadership requires focus and flexibility. It can be very difficult to achieve this if large amounts of client work are taking up time and energy. No matter how well intentioned leaders are, client work will take precedence over important leadership responsibilities; it is ingrained in the professional mindset that the client, the revenue stream, comes first.

One senior partner we interviewed describes how moving away from client work enabled him to focus on his leadership role:

> When I took over the role as senior partner the theory was that I would continue to do client work and business development. But as a corporate lawyer I spent my time doing transactions – they take over your whole life! Leadership requires steady, routine application. You cannot just disappear for a month to do a transaction. I had one transaction that I was in the middle of when I took over the leadership role and that was very difficult, very full on.
>
> Because I took the leadership reins around the time of the financial crisis, I very quickly did less fee-earning work than my predecessor. The balance of my time moved to management. That wasn't a concern to everybody else but it was a concern to me because I liked doing client work. Stepping away from client work wasn't part of the original deal for me but it was ultimately the right thing for me to do for the benefit of the firm.

The experience described above is shared by many of the leaders we interviewed. It is not uncommon for them to miss the thrill of client work and being hands-on with their team. However, it is possible to find other ways to retain valuable client contact; for example, through conducting client relationship reviews with firm-wide key clients, bolstering the team and adding gravitas by attending pitches for high-value work opportunities or by attending client roundtables and other business development events. Retaining this client proximity, without the fixed commitment of fee-earning work makes you a better leader because it prevents your view from becoming too internally focused and hence too far removed from the clients and markets your firm serves.

What happens after your tenure as leader is over? Returning to client work and business development full-time can be tough, especially if you have taken a long pause from fee-earning and have handed over your existing client relationships to others in the firm to manage. As the professional services ecosystem changes, new opportunities arise for former managing partners or other leaders of professional firms. It is now possible to move to in-house roles, take on consultancy roles or become non-executive directors among other opportunities.

It is important to think about your potential exit from leadership as early on as possible. Ask yourself the following questions:

- How long do I want to take on a full-time leadership role for?
- How easy will it be to go back to what I was doing before, or do I need to consider another exit route?
- Where might I be able to apply the skills and competencies I have developed as a leader elsewhere in my firm or in a completely new context?
- How will I know when it is naturally time to look for a new opportunity or challenge?
- What do I need to communicate to others in the firm about my exit intentions and when?

It is not impossible to rebuild a successful practice from scratch. However, as Tina Williams, chair of London law firm Fox Williams, points out, this may mean moving sideways rather than trying to return to the same role you occupied previously:

> I was an international M&A lawyer and clearly that was not compatible with taking on a senior leadership role in the firm. I couldn't put all my leadership responsibilities on hold while I waited for a transaction to close. So I had to step away from M&A after I took the decision to move into leadership. However, I wanted to use the skills learnt from leading the firm and apply that to fee-earning work, so I changed my practice area to working with professional practices. It was a good complement to the skills I developed leading the firm, I had a good handle on what was happening in the legal marketplace and other professional practices as well as an affinity for their strategic and management challenges.

## Manage your time as a leader

Successful leaders accept that, although the potential demands on their time might be infinite, the time that they have is finite. A leader's time is particularly valuable and so should be managed and deployed in a way that creates maximum impact. However, it is important to realize that not every available minute of time is equal. Everybody has times of the day at which they perform better, and times where productivity is lower. An awareness of how you operate is really important for understanding when your 'primetime' slots are.

With a higher degree of self-knowledge, you can structure your day to align important tasks with your primetime slots. Gavin Davies, a corporate and M&A partner at law firm Herbert Smith Freehills, explains how he aligns his tasks to his greatest productivity:

> When I was a trainee, a time management expert demonstrated drawing a day's productivity: 9 am to 9 pm on the horizontal axis, the vertical axis representing high to low productivity, and mapping over that how productivity fluctuates during the day. For me, I start the day off early and strongly, productivity dips a bit after lunch and then I finish strongly later into the evening. Considering the day in this way helped me to identify when best to tackle the hardest tasks and when to set aside time for admin and other less demanding tasks.

Managing time effectively requires constant trade-offs. Successful leaders balance rationing their time with being approachable and available for others who need input. However, sometimes you need to say no and shouldn't feel guilty about that. The next time you are trying to weigh up where to focus your efforts, ask yourself this question: in the next hour what is the most useful thing that I can do to move the firm forward? That could be focusing on clients, business or people leadership but it means deliberately focusing on something.

As the boundaries between work time and private time become increasingly blurred, it is all too easy to accept that spending more time on work demands is a consequence of modern life and a requirement of leadership. However, successful leaders of professional firms know that quality time spent on an activity is often better than unfocused hours trying to balance many competing priorities at one time.

There are many analogies with the world of elite sports. If you put yourself in the shoes of a world-class 100-metre sprinter you would probably accept that:

- The balance of your time between training and competing would be heavily skewed towards training.
- Training would be focused on your ultimate goal (an Olympic gold medal) and interim goals (increasing your world ranking to qualify for Olympic selection).

- Training wouldn't just involve running 100 metres repeatedly, it would focus on all aspects that go into success.

- You would not only focus on physical training, but mental training also.

- You would look after your physical and mental fitness including eating and drinking appropriately, sleeping and resting well, and taking time out for other interests.

- All of the above activities would be planned and delivered with discipline.

Like an elite athlete who consciously plans and trains for success, professional services leaders can maximize the impact of their time by taking a more systematic and mindful approach to planning their routine. This should prevent you getting to the end of a week, month or year only to realize that although you have been busy, you haven't achieved the progress that you had planned or expected.

## Effective diary management

All leaders have a tool to assess how much time they spend on different activities: their diary. But most people only use its basic functionality – to organize meetings – and do not take advantage of its full capabilities. Most electronic diaries enable the user to tag blocks of time with a range of different categories. Setting up a category for each of the four aspects of the Leadership Triangle will allow you to tag meetings and activities as you create them and then use the diary to automate the process of filtering against each tag to find out how you divide up your time. Most applications also allow users to assign a colour to each tag which gives an instant visual picture of balance or imbalance just by looking at your diary's weekly or monthly view.

To create a more complete view of how you spend your time, you need to become disciplined not only to use the diary to map out formal meetings but also to use it as a basic time tracking tool for informal activities, by blocking out time for when you are working on individual tasks.

Any diligent secretary or personal assistant should be able to help you manage your diary in this way if you find it difficult to record the information yourself. However, you need to take ownership personally of reviewing the information to analyse if you are focusing on the right balance of priorities. You might find the following questions a helpful way to assess whether you have the balance correct:

- Do I tend to gravitate towards my comfort zone or I do use my time in ways that push me into unfamiliar territory?
- What activities do I need to stop, dial-down, maintain and dial-up?
- Do I have the right balance between tactical delivery issues versus strategic issues?
- Am I firefighting issues that should be dealt with by others in the firm instead?
- Do I deal with too many things that in reality don't need my input?
- Do I spend enough time creating information or am I too much of a consumer?
- Do I block out enough time to focus on myself as a leader?
- Does the balance of time reflect the type of leader that I want to be?
- Do others understand my leadership priorities? If not, how can I articulate them better so that I can use my time better accordingly?

Undertaking this self-analysis can help you focus your attention and gives you greater confidence about when to say yes and when to delegate. Gavin Davies explains how he uses a similar process to plan his time:

> Every few days I will write down my different responsibilities in the order they are most likely to move forward my practice and the firm: client work, business development efforts and management responsibilities. I find it helps me to see the whole picture of what I am trying to achieve, written down. The challenge to manage all the demands on my time is relentless and listing out the major decisions or activities helps me to identify what is the best use of my time. I could get drawn into initiatives which take me too far away from frontline client work, or which produce little real value for my practice or the firm, so I need to prioritize and constantly revisit those priorities.

One professional services managing partner we interviewed described how spending time reviewing her diary helped her to identify the need to bolster resource in some areas of her team:

> I analysed my diary using a traffic light system to understand how I spent my day and to identify the different tasks that I should be doing, should delegate or should stop doing completely. That has helped me to focus on achieving our five-year plan. It has revealed areas where we need to recruit or upskill other members of the team. For example, we have recruited an additional assistant because I cannot, and should not, be spending lots of my time on the detail of all our sales and marketing campaigns. I need support, somebody to take on the leg work, so I can be out in the market flying the flag as well as beating the drum internally with the team.

## Failure to delegate: the hidden trap for professional services leaders

A common reason for achieving only limited impact as a leader is a reluctance to delegate tasks that could be successfully completed by others in the firm. As you change over to a leadership role, this will necessarily mean leaving certain tasks behind (for example, project managing client matters, being an account lead for a particular client or appraising junior members of your team) and taking on new ones. You need to be confident that your leadership and talent pipeline is well managed so that there are people available to delegate these tasks to in future. This will prevent your work life becoming 'silted up' with activities that you continue doing because you have always done them, rather than because you need to do them. To succeed as a leader you need to free up bandwidth for the things that are important for delivering your strategic goals.

Another leader we interviewed explains how using an external coach helped him to understand the power of effective delegation:

> As I grew the practice I found I was working more and more.
> Ninety hour weeks were not sustainable. So I analysed my diary with a coach. Together we looked at the things somebody else should really be doing that I should stop doing. Even if it was my favourite thing

to do, I agreed not to do it because it wasn't my job to do it anymore. The trouble with being promoted is that sometimes you have to let go of the things you love the most and learn a whole new set of skills.'

James Partridge of law firm Thomson, Snell & Passmore takes an even firmer view about the need for leaders to delegate: 'I have become a ruthless delegator. I now say to people inside and outside the firm that I won't go to boring meetings. I am not prepared to waste my time sitting in badly run meetings. There are some things I just won't go to now because it is not a good use of my time.'

Successful leaders know which activities to delegate and when to lead. One way to understand the balance, is to analyse your leadership role from two perspectives. First, are you a sole participant or part of a team? And second, are you primarily a consumer or a creator of ideas and information? Answers to these two questions, can then be plotted onto a matrix as in Figure 12.1.

**Figure 12.1**   Understanding your leadership balance

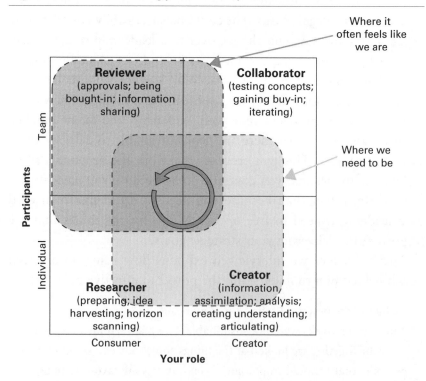

Leaders often find themselves pinned into the top left box: reviewer. In this space it can feel as though your days are filled with other peoples' needs, agendas and requirements, with a limited amount of time to be on the front foot. Successful leaders try to achieve a more balanced approach, whereby they have time to research, develop and test their thoughts, ideas and actions in a more controlled and iterative manner. Achieving this balance, however, relies on effective delegation to maximize time for your own creating thinking. More insights about how to get the most out of others in your team can be found in the People Leadership section.

---

**SUMMARY** Top tips for balancing your time as a leader

### Think hard about fee-earning commitments

Consider what level of chargeable hours you realistically expect to maintain in your leadership role. Many managing partners today have a chargeable hours target of zero. If it is necessary or desirable to maintain some chargeable hours, what strategies will you employ to ensure leadership responsibilities aren't always treated as second-tier priorities? Effective delegation of client commitments and leadership tasks may help you achieve the right balance.

### Plan your possible exit route out of leadership early on

Whether you plan to take on a leadership role for two years or ten years, it is important to think about what happens after you step down. As professional service leaders become younger, many do not see a leadership position as a precursor to retirement but instead as a springboard to new opportunities. Ask yourself how easy it will be to return to full-time fee-earning work in the role you had before or whether a new challenge might provide an opportunity to use your leadership skills in new ways.

### Map out your priorities and performance across the week then organize around your primetime hours

Think like an athlete: know what race you're running, focus on it, use every opportunity as a training opportunity to improve, and make sure you have fun and rest alongside the hard training. Identify your primetime slots and your lulls and prioritize your week around this calendar, focusing on the most important things during the peak times. Carve out time in your diary for various leadership responsibilities, and sufficient time to reflect and think through the challenges on your agenda. Keep this time sacrosanct by avoiding the temptation of being drawn into endless meetings.

### Focus your time planning around decisions, not just activities

When asked what they are doing during the week ahead, most people will list out a string of activities: attending meetings, completing a presentation, emailing a report and so on. Very few people include in their list the decisions or judgements they have to make. As you move into leadership roles you need to stop thinking about time as being merely task-driven to being decision-focused. This way you can plan your hours around the things that will best help you to reach the decisions, and hence achieve the strategic outcomes you need to prioritize.

### Find your leadership 'little big things'

If you are not getting the leadership outcomes or performance that you need or want, step back and review how your time is being spent. What differentiates successful leaders is their ability to identify and use their 'little big things', the small activities or ways of working that turbocharge their leadership impact. What three things could you change in order to get a better result? Test out different options by changing and iterating your leadership approach until you find what works best for you.

# Conclusion

## Put these leadership lessons into action

Now that you have read the previous 12 chapters we hope you have built a deeper understanding of the wide array of challenges confronting professional services leaders within each of the four elements of the Leadership Triangle: business, clients, people and self leadership. We hope you have also become familiar with the guidance and frameworks in the preceding chapters, and that you begin to use these insights to address the particular leadership challenges that manifest themselves within your own organization. We want you to take inspiration from the stories of the leaders we have profiled and to use their wisdom to make yourself a better-informed leader.

At times it might feel that the task ahead is daunting. You may feel you have too many challenges on your agenda and are not sure about what to tackle first. You might also feel that no sooner have you got to grips with one leadership issue than two more come along which require even more of your time and attention. In reality all leaders feel like this, especially at the outset of their leadership tenure. While the professional services leaders we interviewed say their job does not necessarily become easier over time, they all believe that experience has equipped them with greater confidence in their own decision-making and leadership abilities. Self-reflection and coaching can also be incredibly valuable for unlocking and developing latent leadership capabilities along the way.

The leaders we interviewed say they have relished the opportunity to tackle fresh and exciting leadership challenges throughout their career. As we have demonstrated in this handbook, the professional services sector has enjoyed its fair share of disruption and leadership challenges in recent years and there are plenty yet to come. Being a successful leader in a new age of competitive disruption really means being an effective leader of change within your organization; effective leaders are catalysts for change who ensure that their firm keeps pace with their clients and markets. Over the years and decades ahead it is likely that the traditional model of professional services firms as we know it will radically alter; by 2025 professional firms may be structured very differently, serve their clients in new ways and expect very different things of their people. Technology will be more directly involved in how firms serve their clients and as a result will accelerate the pace of change even further. By 2040 things are likely to be just as radically different yet again.

Throughout the previous 12 chapters we have drawn attention to specific examples of how leaders cope with change and disruption within their organizations at the level of both strategy and tactical implementation. At the end of every chapter we summarized five lessons, sixty in total, that provide guidance on common leadership challenges. In this conclusion we highlight 10 further lessons drawn from the collective experience of the leaders we interviewed. These lessons speak to some of the guiding principles successful leaders adopt in order to anticipate and respond effectively to change within their own organization and the professional services sector more widely. These principles will help you to lead your firm through a new age of competitive disruption.

## 1 Keep a balanced perspective on short-term and long-term goals

As a leader it is important to navigate through different time horizons simultaneously. You have a responsibility not only to ensure your firm remains on a profitable footing in the short term, so that it can pay its bills and deliver an appropriate level of profit to partners each year, but also to be a custodian for the firm's longer-term prosperity. As a leader your primary aim should be to leave the firm in a better shape than you found it in at the beginning of your tenure and better prepared to meet the waves of disruption ahead.

In practical terms this means leaders need to pay attention to projects that drive continuous improvement in their firm as well as to initiatives that support more radical innovation. You need to understand how these two time horizons interlock for your firm: a long-term strategic vision should paint a picture of a desired future state for the firm and be underpinned by tangible, short-term actions that are necessary to bring about the desired level of change.

**2 Take time to reflect on your leadership style to maximize your leadership impact**

With multiple demands on your time it is not uncommon to feel that you constantly have your head down moving from one meeting to another, ticking off items on a lengthy to-do list as you go. Having a broad span of responsibilities is inevitable for leaders in professional firms but the most effective leaders take charge of how they spend their time and prioritize accordingly. They also build in sufficient time for reflection about their own leadership performance, style and behaviours.

Effective leaders have a high degree of self-awareness of their own leadership style and how it is perceived by others in their firm. Leading in an age of disruption requires leaders to adapt their leadership style to maximize their impact with different people and in different scenarios. This means you need to think consciously about how best to adapt your leadership approach for different situations without departing from the constant vision and values that underpin your leadership.

**3 Understand your firm's economic model and how it links to client delivery**

Without a sound understanding of how your firm currently makes money, it is almost impossible to make informed decisions about the firm's future strategy. Leaders should focus not just on revenue and billable hours but on how the delivery model adopted by the firm generates profitability. Most professional firms have a portfolio of work types, each with slightly different economic and delivery models, so it is important for leaders to understand how this balance plays out across their span of responsibility. With a good understanding of the economic model of your firm, it will be much clearer which leadership levers will be most effective at increasing profitability and improving how your firm works with clients.

As technology, offshoring and new resourcing models turn traditional professional services delivery models on their head, firms need to adapt their economic model accordingly to take these changes into account. As a leader you need to lay the groundwork for these changes as early as possible and make colleagues aware of the consequences of any changes. Changing your delivery model will not only affect how your firm makes money but will also have a significant impact on the nature of the client experience and the experience of people within your firm.

**4 Collect and communicate a powerful evidence base for your strategic decisions**

As a leader you will undoubtedly have your own hunches and hypotheses about the best strategic direction for your firm but, to convince others, you may need to prove your case with evidence. To build consensus around strategic decisions collect evidence about your firm's clients and markets, people and financial performance and share a summary of the insight with colleagues to enable them to understand the rationale for your decisions. In our experience, weaker leaders confuse consensus building with trying to please everybody, and as a result they either scale back their visionary ideas to the lowest common denominator, or accommodate lots of pet projects that don't align with strategy. Having a robust evidence base will give you greater belief in your strategic vision and the confidence to say no to pet projects when the need arises.

**5 Build organizational commitment for your vision**

Creating strategic change in a professional services environment requires buy-in and a commitment to change. Successful leaders find ways for people publicly to endorse and commit to a shared vision, for example at a partners' conference or as part of a team planning meeting. It is important that colleagues don't just passively accept the change you propose but that they understand and acknowledge the personal impact of the change and what they will do differently as a result of the change.

Where leaders typically come unstuck is in thinking that everybody else in their firm is as far ahead in their thinking as they are; often colleagues will be two steps behind because they won't have had the benefit of dedicated time to think through the implications of the change. Building a commitment to change requires leaders to communicate regularly and to simplify the change into digestible elements. This is why frameworks like the 'plan on a page' are effective at condensing a strategic vision down into simple principles that people can more easily commit to.

**6  Identify potential blockers to change as early as possible**

With any organizational change there will be people who perceive themselves to be winners and people who perceive themselves to be losers. This perception may or may not reflect the reality of the change. There will also be people who struggle to evaluate meaningfully what the change entails for them and, therefore, are likely to be fearful of the unknown. It is important to identify these potential blockers at the outset and to establish a strategy for turning them into advocates of change. Ask yourself: who might be vocal in opposing change and why? Who will need further reassurance and what are their concerns? Often people block change because of a perceived loss of control, loss of access to resources or loss of status. As a leader you need to identify when legitimate concerns can be addressed and when you may need to have difficult conversations with individuals who won't get on board with the change.

**7  Don't get distracted by the multiple demands on your time**

Effective leaders make themselves available and accessible to the people within their firm. However, they also manage their time carefully and assess how much of their time they set aside for different priorities. It is easy to get distracted and find yourself a 'busy fool'. Prioritization is critical for not getting burned out: focus your greatest time and energy on the activities, meetings and initiatives that will move your strategic vision forward and limit the time given to activities that don't fit this criteria.

It is equally important not to overlook activities that will make you a better-informed leader. For example, if you decide to step away from client work as a leader, you may find it helpful to retain some client contact – by undertaking annual relationships reviews for key clients – so that you can hear first-hand how clients describe the experience of working with your firm and the areas where they would like to see greatest improvement.

**8  Delegate where possible and draw on the resources and capabilities that surround you**

Effective leaders know that the success of their strategic vision depends on how well it is implemented, and implementation success depends on working with other people throughout the firm and empowering them to make change happen. Leaders cannot do everything themselves and nor should they. The most successful leaders we have encountered are open about their strengths and limitations, and are aware of when they need to draw on support or delegate to others around them, particularly those with specialist business services skills or expertise in particular markets.

Choosing your top team is a critical factor in leadership success. You want to surround yourself with people whose opinion and judgement you trust – not just people who will tell you what they think you want to hear – and whose capabilities and experiences complement your own. But you also need to be prepared to hear contrary views and factor these into your planning. It is also important to know when to move out beyond your 'inner circle' and consult more widely within the firm. Spending time up front to engage others proactively can pay dividends later on when it comes to relying on others to make change happen.

### 9  Plan your exit or your next leadership challenge

While you need to be absolutely committed to your leadership role to perform successfully, it can be helpful to have an aspiration for the next phase of your career. Whether your leadership tenure is time-limited or not, you should have a view about how long you realistically expect to commit to the role, what you hope to achieve during that time, and what your next step might be. If you anticipate returning to fee-earning full time, it may be necessary to maintain a small amount of fee-earning work during your leadership tenure; if you expect to move on to a completely new challenge, it will probably be distracting to retain fee-earning work. As somebody with experience leading a complex organization like a professional services firm you will have developed highly valuable skills and capabilities that will be transferable to many possible future challenges.

### 10  Enjoy the leadership experience!

Although there are moments when leading a professional firm can seem a painful endeavour, on balance the experience should be exciting and enjoyable. It is not uncommon for people to enter the professions because they have a passion for their profession or business and only later on to discover a passion for leadership, either accidentally or by choice. Whatever your route to leadership, it can be a rewarding experience, not to mention a privilege, to lead an organization in one of the most profitable and dynamic businesses sectors that contribute so much to the smooth functioning of the global economy. When times get tough, refer back to your leadership vision and let that initial sense of possibility and opportunity fill you with the energy and momentum you need to succeed in – and enjoy – your leadership journey.

Our experience investigating professional services leadership has revealed that there are no perfect leaders, nor is there a single ideal model of leadership that all leaders must follow to be successful. This handbook is a guide only, not a prescriptive rule book for success. But one thing has become very clear to us through writing this book: being a successful leader in a new age of competitive disruption requires you to be adaptable to change, open to new possibilities and opportunities as they arise, and not afraid to lead a firm into an unpredictable future. This will necessarily mean changing course somewhat as you go and not sticking too dogmatically to your original strategic plan when external factors change. However, if you maintain a clear sense of direction and a constant vision, others in your firm will follow where you lead. Being adaptable means making trade-offs and switching focus between business, client, people and self leadership as priorities change from time to time.

It is the adaptable nature of professional services leadership that makes the sector resilient in the face of change, and an exciting environment in which to hold a leadership role. As a leader you play a central role in shaping this uncertain future, whether you are just starting out on your leadership journey or reaching that journey's end. With so much disruption and change afoot, the opportunity to leave a leadership legacy is great: ultimately you want to be known not as the leader who managed inevitable decline in your firm but as the leader who set the firm on a course to future prosperity.

# INDEX

Note: **bold** page numbers indicate figures; *italic* numbers indicate tables.